MW00440856

Also by Harriet and Shirley

Prayer Warrior Confessions
Glimpses of Prayer, a devotional
Glimpses of the Savior, a devotional

By Harriet

Prayer, It's Not About You

By Shirley

Study Guide on Prayer

Glimpses of God

a winter devotional for women

Harriet E. Michael
Shirley Crowder

Shirley Crowder
Psalm 143:8

Dedication

We dedicate this devotional to
the godly men and women
who have discipled and mentored
us throughout our lives and particularly to:
Donna Pavkovich and Nancy Ogle,
Harriet's Bible study leaders
at Precepts and Bible Study Fellowship
who have taught her much,
and
Dr. Howard Eyrich,
Shirley's dear brother-in-Christ,
mentor, and friend,
who has taught, prayed for,
encouraged, and advised her,
and with whom it has been her joy
to minister alongside.

Remember your leaders,
who spoke the word of God to you.
Consider the outcome of their way of life
and imitate their faith.
Hebrews 13:7

Table of Contents

Creator God made the world in which we live. He placed the moon and stars in the sky, the rivers and oceans on the earth. He also created seasons throughout the year. Each season is defined by specific features or attributes that are common, although the degree varies depending on where a person lives.

In the same way that nature's seasons serve a purpose on earth, so do the seasons in our spiritual lives. God provides, cares for, and sustains the earth. In His faithfulness, He does the same for us. Our responsibility is to be obedient to God's commands in Scripture and to cling to the truth that God is in control.

This book focuses on the season of winter, both calendar and spiritual. During our spiritual winters, we might feel stuck or dormant. Sometimes God might even seem far away. It is definitely a time of waiting, resting, and reflecting. We must cease striving and find peace in the truth of God's sovereign mercy, grace, love, and care for His children.

We pray that as you read and meditate upon the Scripture passages and truths in each devotional that you will catch glimpses of God in and through everything around you. How has He provided for you? How is He protecting you? How is He teaching you?

Chapter 1
The Holly and the Ivy

Day 1: The Holly and the Ivy

by Harriet
Read: James 4:13-15

*Teach us to number our days, that we may
gain a heart of wisdom.*
Psalm 90:12 (NIV)

Have you ever read the lyrics to the old Christmas carol, "The Holly and the Ivy?" If you are like me, the tune is probably more familiar than the lyrics. But if you have taken the time to read the words, you probably wondered about them. The holly is mentioned repeatedly but the ivy only in the refrain, with a conclusion drawn that the holly is better. How strange. And why are we using it at the start of this book?

A little research turned up some helpful information as to what the words mean. The holly represents Jesus. The words in the various verses mention the holly's white (lily) flower which symbolizes Jesus' purity, the red berry His blood, and the holly's thorns His crown of thorns. So, of course, Jesus is better than anything to which He could be compared. But why did the writer use the ivy for the comparison rather than something else?

The writer's reason for mentioning ivy is much more difficult to figure out, and much of what I found in my research simply pointed to the fact that both holly and ivy were often used at Christmastime to decorate homes in the 17th-18th centuries when this carol may have been written. People then had to decorate with whatever they could find, so the evergreen holly and ivy were used to brighten things up and bring winter cheer.

We chose these two images to start off our book because they seem to so perfectly illustrate this first chapter, devotions for a time of transition between the holidays and the new calendar year, the old and the new.

The holly represents Jesus, and the ivy stands for us. Holly also represents the beauty of the year and years that are behind us, while the ivy seems so perfect for days yet to unfold. These days sprawl out ahead of us like ivy climbing on a tree, evergreen and endlessly winding where it will. At least, they seem that way as they lie in front of us and we cannot see the end of them. They are not endless, though. Someday our lives, the way we lived, the things we did, and the ways in which we impacted others for good or for bad will be a closed book. Our story will be over and our chance to change things will have passed.

In today's key verse, the psalmist asks God to "show me, LORD, my life's end and the number of my days; let me know how fleeting my life is" (Psalm 39:4 NIV). David is asking God to teach him to remember that his days are not endless so that he might seek after wisdom.

This may seem like a somber note on which to begin, and surely other sections will be lighter and more encouraging. But what could be more important at this time of looking back at the old year and ahead to the new one, than to learn to number our days and to gain the wisdom and insight that comes with that understanding?

Prayer: Gracious Heavenly Father, like the old hymn reminds us, "You are our help in ages past and our hope for years to come." In this time of transition between the old year and the new one, help us to learn to seek wisdom. Bless us in the year ahead that we may apply that wisdom. In Jesus' name, Amen.

Thought for the Day: Like the holly and ivy, the days behind us and the days ahead are beautiful and beckoning. May we remember God in them all.

Day 2: No Returns!

by Shirley
Read: Romans 7:1-7

*Thanks be to God for his
indescribable gift!*
2 Corinthians 9:15 (NKJV)

Driving home from work one day after Christmas I saw a church marquee that read, "The Gift of Jesus Christ: No Returns!" I could not get that saying out of my mind. All night long and for the next several days I mulled it over and over in my mind. This marquee evoked three primary thoughts.

My first thought was that the gift of Jesus Christ is one we do not want to return. Yet, at times when we *feel* life is not being fair to us, we may develop a desire to *return* His gift. In that way, we are treating Jesus like a Christmas present that we play with for a little while and then get tired of, disappointed with, or simply lose interest in altogether. Guard against this desire by being diligent to consistently read, study, memorize, meditate, and contemplate upon the word of God.

Psalm 1 gives a good picture of what it means to walk with God and to learn and obey His word. The word of God forms the basis of a Christ-follower's life, and the better we know that word, the better equipped we are to live each day enjoying and depending upon Him.

The Christ-follower "delights in the law of the Lord" (Psalm 1:2)—his heart responds to God's word. That delight propels him to learn and obey that word and leads him to meditate upon that word day and night. Through meditation, our hearts and minds are saturated and transformed (Romans 12:2).

I could also have read this marquee to mean that Jesus Christ will never return to earth. This, of course, is NOT true! Scripture tells us that the baby Jesus who was born in a manger and died on the cross as our Savior to redeem us was resurrected, ascended to heaven, and will surely return to earth one day! "For the Lord himself will descend from heaven with a cry of command, with the voice of an archangel, and with the sound of the trumpet of God. And the dead in Christ will rise first. Then we who are alive, who are left, will be caught up together with them in the clouds to meet the Lord in the air, and so we will always be with the Lord" (1 Thessalonians 4:16-17).

Thinking about Jesus and the word "return" made me think about our need to return to Jesus in repentance of the sin that separates us from Him. We need to humbly come to Him for salvation as Psalm 62:1 (NIV) tells us, "Truly my soul finds rest in God; my salvation comes from him." Once we are saved, we must continually "return" to Him for forgiveness of the sins we commit. Lamentations 5:21 (NKJV) says, "Turn us back to You, O LORD, and we will be restored; renew our days as of old." King David, a man after God's own heart, prayed, "Create in me a clean heart, O God, and renew a steadfast spirit within me" (Psalm 51:10 NKJV).

As our thoughts and activities are focused on the Christmas season, remember to cherish the precious gift of Jesus Christ, to look forward to the return of Christ, and to return to Jesus.

Prayer: Heavenly Father, thank You for the gift of Jesus Christ, our Savior and Lord. Help us learn how to love and serve Him better. In His name, we pray, Amen.

Thought for the Day: Remember and appreciate the gift of Jesus Christ anew each day and live your life preparing and watching for His second return, all the while making sure you humbly return to Him.

Day 3: Harmattan

by Harriet
Read: Job 10:8-12

For he knows our frame;
he remembers that we are dust.
Psalm 103:14

This time of year is a special time in Nigeria, the country where Shirley and I grew up. It is the middle of the dry season right now, a special mini-season called *Harmattan*. Nigeria is a country on the west coast of Africa just beneath the Sahara Desert. Christmas and New Year in Nigeria fall on the calendar at the same time as Harmattan.

The Harmattan is a dry and dusty West African trade wind. It blows southwest from the Sahara Desert into the Gulf of Guinea between the end of November and the middle of March. Humidity is extremely low, and the heavy amount of dust in the air can sometimes severely limit visibility and block the sun for days. It has a similar effect to that of a heavy fog.

Against this backdrop, we celebrated Christmas and New Year. My father used to say that he liked the fact that Christmas came in the middle of Harmattan. In America, everything would be stark, cold, and dreary this time of year, with the trees bare and the air full of winter's chill. In the middle of this otherwise dreary time, Christians celebrate the birth of the Savior with ornamented and brightly lit Christmas trees, gifts, good food, and Christmas cheer. Likewise, in Nigeria, when the world is dry and dusty, and all the leaves and grass are a dreary brown, Christians are celebrating the joyous birth of their Savior with songs and good cheer.

Growing up, I knew Harmattan to be a season of dry air and extreme dust. When I was just a baby, I had very thin, wispy, blond hair. During the Harmattan season, the static electricity from the dry blowing air caused my hair to stand on end most of the time and my family fondly called me "Harriet the Harmattan cat" because my hair looked like the hair on the back of cats when they arch in fear or anger. As I got older, and my hair thickened and behaved, I became accustomed to this time of year when dust accumulated on our furniture overnight and covered the trees in the outside world around me.

I knew what dust was like. It formed quickly and could be shaken off the trees or wiped away just as quickly. The Bible tells us we are like that. James 4:14 compares our lives to a vapor, appearing for a little while and then vanishing.

In this time of year, when we reflect on the previous year while also focusing on the upcoming one, what can we learn from our past? How can we apply that knowledge to our future choices? In the northern hemisphere, we have holly and ivy to remind us of the past and future of our lives compared to Jesus' life. In Africa, we had Harmattan to remind us of the brevity of life, that from dust we came and to dust we will return. Maybe today's devotion should have been entitled "Holly, Ivy, and Harmattan."

Our key verse gives us some good news, though. God knows that we are but flesh. We are mere humans fraught with human frailty. Yet He chose to work His marvelous plan for His creation using us—humans—whose lives are so short in comparison to eternity. What does He have in store for you in the coming new year?

Prayer: Loving Father, You have created us for a purpose here today, and in the days to come. Use us in the time You have given us to glorify You. In Jesus' name, Amen.

Thought for the Day: "Teach us to number our days, that we may gain a heart of wisdom" (Psalm 90:12 NIV).

Day 4: Holiday Letdown

by Shirley
Read: Psalm 42

*Why are you cast down, O my soul, and
why are you in turmoil within me?
Hope in God; for I shall again praise him,
my salvation and my God.*
Psalm 42:11

Since early November, most of us have been keeping a frantic pace. We have holiday decorating to complete, family gatherings to plan, holiday cooking to do, parties to attend, countless gifts to purchase and wrap, choir presentations to attend along with school pageants and numerous other activities that fill our calendars.

Following the excitement and celebrations of the holidays, the first of the year seems dull by comparison. We return to our regular schedules after the new year begins and face our old routine and a mountain of holiday bills, all while the coldness of winter encroaches, sometimes giving rise to the holiday letdown.

A sadness begins to creep in, and that often leads to us to disliking our mundane tasks we must do. If we allow our holiday letdown to go unchecked, we will quickly spiral into a sense of hopelessness.

Remember, King David, whom God called "a man after my heart" (Acts 13:22), suffered various types of letdowns throughout his life. Many of the psalms he wrote are outpourings of his heart to God while he struggled with his emotions.

The only way we can come out of our period of holiday letdown, or a letdown or disappointment of any sort, is to "be transformed by the renewal of [our] mind" (Romans 12:2) through the Holy Spirit-inspired Bible. We can begin praising God and giving thanks for our blessings, which are innumerable. As we read Scripture, we are reminded that we can't trust our emotions, but we can trust God. We must continually remind ourselves that we "know that for those who love God all things work together for good, for those who are called according to his purpose" (Romans 8:28). Granted, we can't always see the "good" in whatever we are experiencing and feeling, but we know that God is at work in and through everything that we experience to make us more into His image.

Sometimes we need to, "Be still, and know that [He is] God" (Psalm 46:10), which can lead us to remember that, "On him we have set our hope that he will deliver us again" (2 Corinthians 1:10).

Sometimes our reading, praying, meditating, and contemplating upon Scripture brings about the Holy Spirit's conviction of sin in our lives (John 16:13), and we must confess and repent of that sin, and walk in the freedom of God's forgiveness.

We can have hope because we know that, "The steadfast love of the LORD never ceases; his mercies never come to an end; they are new every morning; great is [His] faithfulness" (Lamentations 3:22-23). And 1 John 4:9-10 (NIV) reminds us that, "This is how God showed his love among us: He sent his one and only Son into the world that we might live through him. This is love: not that we loved God, but that he loved us and sent his Son as an atoning sacrifice for our sins."

Focusing our hearts on God brings His peace (Philippians 4:7) and renewed strength (Isaiah

40:29-31) because we know, "God shall supply all [our] need according to his riches in glory by Christ Jesus" (Philippians 4:19). Any time my mom would hear or talk about God supplying all our needs, she would say, "My Heavenly Father owns everything, so what do I have to be depressed or worried about?"

So, when the holiday letdown begins to creep in, remember to focus your heart on God—our only source of hope in any situation.

Prayer: Gracious Heavenly Father, when depression creeps into our lives, help us come to You for help. Thank You for loving us and leaving us Your word and Your Holy Spirit to help us when we need You. In Jesus' name, Amen.

Thought for the Day: "God is our refuge to whom we may flee, and in whom we may be safe and think ourselves so; secure upon good grounds" (Matthew Henry, about Psalm 46:1).

Day 5: How Do You Feel?

by Harriet
Read: 1 Peter 1:8-12

*But you are a chosen people, a royal
priesthood, a holy nation,
God's special possession, that you may
declare the praises
of him who called you out of darkness
into his wonderful light.*
1 Peter 2:9 (NIV)

How do you feel today? The excitement of
Christmas is behind you and now you are facing a
new year. Maybe you have clean-up work ahead of
you—decorations to put back in boxes and store
away for another year, wrapping paper and other
remnants of friends and family strewn all over the
place needing to be picked up, or work waiting for
you at your desk when you return to your job.

Maybe you have other things weighing on you.
The holidays and the days that follow prove to be
difficult for many. Are you tired and lonely? Are
you weighed down by the demands and troubles of

this world? Does just going back to work feel overwhelming? Does it almost feel like a dark cloud surrounds you and accompanies you wherever you go, like cartoonists sometimes depict?

Or maybe you don't feel bad at all. Maybe, in fact, you woke up this morning feeling great. The demands of the holidays are behind you and you feel ready to face the new year. Just how good did you feel? Maybe you thought to yourself, "I feel like I'm royalty! I feel like a priest!"

Well, that's what the Scriptures say we are if we are believers in Jesus Christ. According to the passages we read today, we are a royal priesthood, a holy nation, a chosen people. We are God's own possession. Isn't that marvelous! Do we ever pause to remember this? The truth of who you and I are in Christ transcends our earthly problems.

Did you notice the purpose clause in the verse? *Why* are we a chosen people, a royal priesthood, a holy nation? It is so that we can proclaim the excellence of Him who called us out of darkness. So … kiss that dark cloud goodbye! You and I have been called out of darkness and into God's marvelous light! Keep that in mind as the new year approaches. Walk in that light and enjoy the warmth of His love. It is better than the sunniest summer day!

How do you feel now? No matter how you answer that question, the truth of who you are in Christ remains. And that's enough to bring you joy regardless of your circumstances.

Prayer: Gracious Heavenly Father, who chose us to be Your own possession, help us to remember who we are in Christ. Make us to conduct ourselves in a manner that is fitting for the holy nation You have declared us to be. Thank You for calling us out of darkness and into Your marvelous light! In Jesus' name, Amen.

Thought for the Day: Remember who you are and the purpose for which you have been chosen today, and in the days to come. Find opportunities today to proclaim God's excellence to your friends, family, or acquaintances.

Chapter 2

New Beginnings

Day 1: Give Me Jesus

by Shirley
Read: Psalm 143:8-11

*Let the morning bring me word
of your unfailing love,
for I have put my trust in you.
Show me the way I should go,
for to you I entrust my life.*
Psalm 143:8 (NIV)

Mornings are great! Each morning when you awaken, a new day awaits and with that new day we have the promise that God's mercies are "new every morning" (Lamentations 3:22-23). Yet, we often don't even want to open our eyes and start that new day.

Today's passage tells us how David prepared himself to hear from God so that he would be able to follow God throughout his day.

How do you greet the new day? A beautiful African American spiritual is, "In the Morning When I Rise (Give Me Jesus)." This prayer reflects the thoughts of the hardships slaves had to endure, and their confidence in Jesus Christ as their Savior who would give them the strength to bear whatever they experienced, and who made a way for them to spend eternity in heaven worshiping God the Father.

Think about it. Many slaves had no earthly possessions they could call their own and they likely longed for some earthly conveniences and pleasures. Yet they understood that without Jesus Christ, no earthly possessions, conveniences, or pleasures offered them any help or hope.

The first verse of this spiritual expresses their understanding that their relationship with Jesus was all they needed. It set the tone for their day as they sang this prayer:

In the morning, when I rise,
In the morning, when I rise,
In the morning, when I rise,
Give me Jesus.

The refrain continued as they sang:

Give me Jesus. Give me Jesus,
You may have all this world,
But give me Jesus.

This hymn reminds us of the importance of beginning each day spending time with Jesus in prayer, Bible reading, studying, meditating, and contemplating in order to focus our hearts and minds upon Him. Through this time with God we will "be strengthened with power through His Spirit in [our] inner being, so that Christ may dwell in [our] hearts through faith" and be "rooted and grounded in love" (Ephesians 3:14-17). As we read or sing the words, we remember that Christ Jesus Himself is what we should want the most.

Fanny J. Crosby wrote a beautiful hymn, "Give Me Jesus," that echoes these biblical truths. The last verse expresses another prayer:

Take the world, but give me Jesus;
In His cross my trust shall be,
Till, with clearer, brighter vision,
Face to face my Lord I see.

The refrain explains the basis of our trust in Jesus:

> Oh, the height and depth of mercy!
> Oh, the length and breadth of love!
> Oh, the fullness of redemption,
> Pledge of endless life above!

Both of these hymns remind me of a C. S. Lewis quote from *"Mere Christianity:"* "[God] Himself is the fuel our spirits were designed to burn, or the food our spirits were designed to feed on. There is no other."

In Mark 8:35-36 we find out that life is valuable, and as Christ-followers we must willingly give up our lives, knowing that we may lose our life for now, yet gain it again through eternal life.

Prayer: Heavenly Father, thank You for each new morning You grant us. Help us learn to come to You in the morning so that our hearts are focused upon You and we are sensitive to Your leading for that day. Give us a passion to know You more and want nothing but You. In Jesus' name, Amen.

Thought for the Day: Be diligent to put your trust in God each morning as you seek His leading for your day.

Day 2: Mornings

by Harriet
Read: 1 Samuel 15:10-13, 16

*Early in the morning Samuel got up and
went to meet Saul ...*
1 Samuel 15:12a (NIV)

Are you a morning person or a night one? Personally, I'm a morning person so, naturally, this chapter's theme of New Beginnings made me think of mornings since they are the beginning of each new day. I love mornings! They always have a freshness to me as if they hold a secret promise of great things that might happen as the day unfolds.

Some years ago, I was researching and writing *Prayer: It's Not About You.* As I researched, I made my way through the Scripture—from Genesis to Revelation. In doing this, I came across passage after passage where one Bible character or another rises early in the morning to do something God had called them to do that day, or to seek God in some way. Here are some examples, just to list a few:

Abraham rose early the day he planned to offer Isaac as a sacrifice, according to Genesis 22:3. He again rose early the day after Sodom and Gomorrah were destroyed, hurrying to a place where he could look down on the cities to see if they had been destroyed (Genesis 19:27-28).

Joshua rose early to travel to the Jordan before he crossed over (Joshua 3:1).

David rose early to obey his father Jesse and take supplies to his brothers in battle (1 Samuel 17:20).

God instructed Moses to rise early when he was to stand before Pharaoh and tell him to let God's people go and of course, we assume Moses obeyed (Exodus 8:20).

And on and on it goes. If you look for this pattern in Scripture, you will find it. So, what's the lesson here? Is this bad news for people like my husband, who tend to stay up late and then do not care so much for mornings, people who need a little extra time and maybe a cup of coffee, before they can even begin to embrace the new day? I don't think so. I don't think the biblical point here is to love mornings as much as it is to get on with whatever God has for you to do in life. In the Bible times, before electricity, if they were going to apply themselves to whatever action they felt God had asked of them, they'd better not waste any daylight. They had better get on with it.

Today, doing what God has asked of you may require staying up late instead of rising early. But the point remains—embrace the day! Or rather, embrace what God is calling you to do today, and get busy doing it, whether that means getting up early or sleeping in because you stayed up late the night before working on what God called you to do.

Me? I prefer getting up early. I love mornings. Scripture has a special blessing for mornings in Lamentations 3:22-23 when it says, "God's mercies are new every morning, and his compassions never fail." I wake up most mornings keenly aware of those new mercies as I see the sun streaking through my window as the morning breaks.

It's the start of a new year. What has God been nudging you to do?

Prayer: Heavenly Father, give me a willing heart

and eager attitude to do what You have prepared for me to do today. Make me a person who is ready and willing to rise early and be about my Father's business. In Your Son's name, Amen.

Thought for the Day: Get up! It's a new day and God has much for you to do!

Day 3: Joy Unspeakable

by Shirley
Read: 1 Peter 1:1-9

*Though you have not seen him, you love
him. Though you do not now see him,
you believe in him and rejoice with joy
that is inexpressible and filled with glory,
obtaining the outcome of your faith, the
salvation of your souls.*
1 Peter 1:8-9

Happiness and joy are not the same thing.
Happiness is a response to things going on around
us, and it usually indicates that good—as we
perceive it—things are happening. Joy is a response
to the indwelling of the Holy Spirit. The source of
joy is God. Scripture tells us that it is a fruit of the
Spirit given to all Christ-followers.

Sadly, we often live joyless lives. When we
come to Christ and begin to know Him and
understand joy—what joy is and how to respond in
joy to God—we will choose to live a life of joy.

Peter tells us that Christ-followers can live

lives of "unspeakable joy" (1 Peter 1:8), a joy so extraordinary that we cannot adequately describe it.

I can't talk about the joy of the Lord without thinking of my mom. She is always the example I use of a person who exhibited "the joy of the Lord." She walked joyfully through her life—even through the hard and life-threatening situations she faced—exuding God's joy because she knew her Savior was in control of everything. This type of joy is not dispensed only to super saints; it is part of the fruit of the Spirit that God gives to every Christ-follower.

The degree to which that joy manifests itself in and through a Christ-follower is directly proportionate to the amount of time spent communicating with God through prayer, Bible reading, studying, meditating, and contemplating.

As Christ-followers we experience joy in our relationship with Jesus Christ. Paul tells us to "rejoice in the Lord" (Philippians 4:4). Okay, what does that mean? It means that the truth of who Jesus is—what He did for us on the cross and in His resurrection, what He is doing for us presently, and what He will do for us in the future—has an overwhelming effect on us. It can completely transform us. Regardless of what happens to us or around us, God's joy resounds in our hearts because He is the focus of our joy.

Barney E. Warren wrote a wonderful hymn, "Joy Unspeakable," that is based on 1 Peter 1:8. Warren reminds us of God's all-complete grace, how He supplies all our needs, the pleasure of our salvation and living in His grace. The wonderful chorus reminds us that all of the words that have ever been spoken to describe the joy of the Lord have only scratched the surface in describing that joy!

It is joy unspeakable and full of glory,
Full of glory, full of glory;
It is joy unspeakable and full of glory,
Oh, the half has never yet been told.

The last verse describes the joy of the Lord so well when it says:

I have found the joy no tongue can tell,
How its waves of glory roll;

It is like a great o'erflowing well,
Springing up within my soul.

That "great o'erflowing well springing up within [your] soul" allows you to experience the unspeakable joy of the Lord. If you are not experiencing that unspeakable joy, pray and ask the Holy Spirit to restore that joy in your heart. If unconfessed sin is blocking that joy, be quick to confess that sin, ask for forgiveness, and walk in the freedom that allows God's unspeakable joy to flow freely in and through your life.

Prayer: Our gracious Heavenly Father, we thank You for the gift of joy You give us when we are born again. Teach us to love You more and to realize that joy is not just a feeling, but a response to Your greatness, power, presence, glory, mercy, and grace. In Jesus' name, Amen.

Thought for the Day: "The LORD is my strength and my shield; my heart trusts in him, and he helps me. My heart leaps for joy, and with my song I praise him" (Psalm 28:7 NIV).

Day 4: Bath Time!

by Harriet
Read: Hebrews 9:11-14

*Create in me a pure heart, O God, and
renew a steadfast spirit within me.*
Psalm 51:10 (NIV)

Truth be told, all of my children loved bath time. I've heard stories about how little boys were supposed to detest taking baths, but that just wasn't the case for my three sons, or my daughter, either. Now, it's true, they all loved playing outside and never seemed to mind getting dirty, but they didn't mind baths, either. Maybe it was because I tried to make it fun for them. They had bath toys, bubble bath, capsules that made the water turn colors, and the most fun of all—bath crayons! I still have a precious picture of one of my sons, a chubby blond, sitting in a tub full of bubbles with a blue crayon in his hand, blue marks all over the wall, and a blue face up to his eyes.

I love a long soak in a hot tub of water too, especially in the cold winter. But what I like best is the clean feeling after the bath. How well I can remember this with my children when they were toddlers. Toddlers can get pretty stinky by day's end. But after their evening bath, with freshly washed hair, and clean pajamas on, they were the epitome of adorable babies.

The Bible talks about becoming clean and new again in our hearts and souls. The catalyst for cleaning our hearts is not soap, but rather the blood of Jesus Christ shed on the cross for us. Today's passage makes that so clear when it says, "The blood of goats and bulls and the ashes of a heifer sprinkled on those who are ceremonially unclean sanctify them so that they are outwardly clean. How much more, then, will the blood of Christ, who through the eternal Spirit offered himself unblemished to God, cleanse our consciences from acts that lead to death, so that we may serve the living God!"

Verse 13 refers to the sacrifices the people of God were required to make in Old Testament times, juxtaposing that with the once-for-all sacrifice

Jesus made for those who would believe in Him.

My analogy of getting our bodies clean as compared to having our hearts cleansed breaks down in one area—when our bodies are bathed, they get dirty again, but once we are washed in Jesus' blood, our souls are saved for all eternity. Even so, we still need cleansing of our daily sins through repentance. Believers need to wash in God's word daily to keep our hearts pure and keep us serving God.

My Bible study leader spoke about this some weeks ago. She asked, "You wouldn't want to go weeks or months without a shower, would you? So, would you go weeks or months without renewing and refreshing your hearts through Scripture study?"

This struck a chord with me. Some days I might think I am too busy to have my personal devotions, but I never think I am too busy to clean up and brush my teeth and hair before starting my day. Likewise, bathe in God's word, immerse yourself in the purifying, heart-cleansing word every day.

Prayer: Heavenly Father, right now it's the start of a new year. As we give thought to fresh starts and new beginnings, help us to remember that You graciously give us a fresh start and a new beginning every morning. Forgive our sins, cleanse our hearts through Your word, and show us what You have for us in this new beginning. In Jesus' name, Amen.

Thought for the Day: Get up, clean your body and heart and get ready to face a new day!

Day 5: Awake, My Soul

by Shirley
Read: Jeremiah 12:1-5

If you have raced with men on foot,
and they have wearied you,
how will you compete with horses?
And if in a safe land you are so trusting,
what will you do in the thicket of the
Jordan?
Jeremiah 12:5

As the coldness and darkness of winter drag on, it is easy for us to lose heart and not want to keep on going. In the same manner, when the trials of everyday life come, we sometimes find ourselves overwhelmed.

Years ago, I was at the beach with friends. One evening as I sat near the pool watching children play, a boy who looked about seven slowly made his way down the steps into the shallow end with his dad just a few inches in front of him coaxing him into deeper waters by saying, "Come on Jerry, you can do it. I'm right here to help you."

Jerry slowly moved closer to the deep end. As he took the step that brought the water just under his chin, another boy did a cannonball and landed about two feet away, sending deep rippling waves throughout the pool. You guessed it, those waves caused Jerry's head to submerge under water, which of course scared him. He yelled, "Help! I'm drowning!" His dad reached out and easily lifted Jerry, so his head was completely above water.

The next morning, I sat on a perch beside the walkway down to the beach while I drank a cup of coffee. I heard a boy arguing with his dad. When I turned around, I recognized Jerry and his dad. The boy was pouting that his dad wouldn't let him go down by himself and swim in the ocean. His dad said they had to go to the pool and let his baby sister play, so Jerry would have to be happy playing in the pool until his dad could go into the ocean with him. Jerry's pouting and arguing soon turned to crying.

His dad said, "You thought you were drowning yesterday in the pool when a little wave splashed over your head and you were standing on both feet. What are you going to do when a big wave comes along and knocks you off your feet and you are totally under water?"

Jerry's dad was asking his son the same question God asked Jeremiah in today's key passage. The context of the passage finds the prophet Jeremiah abandoned by his friends who have become his enemies because he prophesied for God. They did not like being told they were going to be destroyed. In fact, the people in his hometown hated him so much they were plotting to kill him.

Jeremiah asked God why these wicked people prospered (Jeremiah 12:1), and God did not really answer his question. Instead, he basically asked, "If you can't deal with the ordinary things in everyday life, how are you going to deal with the very difficult and devastating things you will likely face in the future?"

Like the dad who reached out to lift his son above the water, our Heavenly Father stands ready to give us the strength to withstand, regardless of how dire the situation in which we find ourselves. But what is our responsibility here? We must know Jesus Christ as our Savior and Lord, our only hope and source of strength. We must train ourselves to trust in God alone to carry us through the ordinary things by being consistent in prayer, Bible reading, studying, meditating, and contemplating, and obeying His commands. This training increases our faith and teaches us to be ready so that when the difficult and devastating things come, we will be able to stand firm in our faith and trust in God (Matthew 24:13).

We stretch our muscles when we wake up in the morning and before we exercise. A Harvard Medical School article I read some time ago said stretching muscles is important in helping them remain "flexible, strong, and healthy." It goes on to say that not stretching our muscles puts us at risk for injury.

In the ordinary things, our spiritual muscles are stretched and conditioned so that we are flexible and strong when the difficult and devastating things come. This stretching teaches us to persevere and trust God in every situation.

Philip Doddridge wrote the words of "Awake, My Soul, Stretch Every Nerve," sung to the tune of "While Shepherds Watched Their Flock by Night." I love the imagery in this hymn!

Awake, my soul, stretch every nerve,
And press with vigor on;
A heav'nly race demands thy zeal,
And an immortal crown.

This hymn is a call for our souls to awaken, stretch, and press on throughout the day, despite the ordinary or difficult and devastating things we face.

Prayer: Gracious Heavenly Father, we know we do not have the strength to endure all the things that may come into our lives. Help us be diligent to prepare our hearts so we will call upon You and trust You to strengthen us to stand strong in every situation that comes into our lives. In Jesus' name, Amen.

Thought for the Day: Are you creating routines of trust that will sustain you during the difficulties that are sure to come into your life?

Chapter 3

Epiphany

Day 1: What is Epiphany?

by Harriet

Read: Isaiah 40:1-5

*Prepare the way for the Lord, make
straight paths for him.*
Mark 1:3b (NIV)

What is Epiphany, anyway? Have you ever wondered about that? I did, most of my life. If you are like me, you can relate to not fully understanding what Epiphany is. I grew up hearing the term at church every January, but my denomination tended to just mention it and not celebrate it in any special way, so I remained confused as to what the holiday really was all about. As it turns out, that confusion is warranted. If I were to ask five different Christians in five different denominations, over several centuries, what they thought Epiphany was, I would likely get five different answers. Most would say it is a celebration of the time the wise men visited Jesus, but after that, there are many differences in how it is celebrated, when it is celebrated, and what it is all about.

Epiphany is also sometimes called "Three Kings Day" or the "Twelfth Day of Christmas" or just "Twelfth Night." Depending on the group, it is celebrated on January 6, or January 19, or from January 6 through the beginning of Lent. And though the Magi visit is indeed a part of it, the real focus is on the fact that the Magi's search for Jesus represents the world as a whole—the Gentiles—learning about Jesus. Thus, its broader meaning is the celebration of the gospel being presented to the world. Because of this broader meaning, Epiphany celebrations can be centered around the gospel, or focus on Jesus' baptism, life, and ministry, as well as be a celebration of worship, and the establishment of the church.

Sadly, as has happened with so many Christian holidays, people through the ages have added practices and traditions that have little resemblance to what the holiday is really about. Like Santa Claus and his elves at Christmas and the Easter bunny at Easter, Epiphany celebrations through the centuries have often included practices such as children leaving out shoes in which to collect toys, cakes with a tiny baby Jesus hidden in them, priests throwing crosses into a body of water with men diving in, racing to be the first to retrieve it. Also, like the other extraneous practices, these, too, sort of leave people scratching their heads as to how the traditions could possibly have anything to do with the actual meaning of the holiday.

Nonetheless, the celebration of Epiphany is part of the liturgical, or church, calendar as a special time when we can stop and think about Jesus Christ and His gospel. He was fully God, yet fully man. He was born of a virgin and grew in wisdom, strength, and favor with God and man. Christ was baptized, had a ministry of teaching, preaching, and healing, and then bore our sins when He willingly gave up His life on the cross. Finally, He rose victoriously, establishing and redeeming His church, His bride.

Our key verse today, "Prepare the way for the Lord," includes words from John the Baptist which are still pertinent today. Now we too need to prepare the way for Jesus in our hearts and lives, and we need to tell others about Him.

Prayer: Lord, prepare our hearts to receive You. Lead us and change us into the people You want us to be. Then give us a passion for telling others about You. In Your name, Amen.

Thought for the Day: Jesus lived and died for you and me! When He established His church, He grafted us in.

Day 2: Wise Men

by Harriet
Read: Matthew 2:1-12

*Where is the one who has been born
king of the Jews?
We saw his star when it rose
and have come to worship him.*
Matthew 2:2b (NIV)

Most of us are familiar with the Christmas story characters—Mary, Joseph, the baby Jesus, shepherds, angels, and of course the three wise men, also called Magi. But what is really known about the Magi, and how do we know it? How many were there, really? What were their names? Were they just wise men or were they kings?

The only things we can say for certain are those details that are included in the biblical accounts because we know the Bible is true. Thus, all we know for sure is what we read in Matthew 2 since they are not mentioned in the other gospel accounts. Rather than recount it, I will share other interesting information about the mystery of the Magi.

It is quite likely they came from a Persian group known as the Magi that had been founded by Daniel after he received the Prophecy of Seventy Weeks from the angel Gabriel (Daniel 9:30). They had been taught to look for a star, though it is not known whether this was through another unrecorded revelation, or if it is the star mentioned in Numbers 24:17.

It is also not known how many Magi there were. Three are assumed because they brought three gifts, but it is likely there were more. Were they kings? Sort of. Matthew calls them wise men, or astrologers from the east. Magi from Persia, whom they are assumed to be, were considered royalty. This is consistent with a prophecy in Psalm 72:10-11, which talks of the kings of Sheba and Seba bringing gifts. Their gifts were the type of gifts only royalty would be able to offer.

We also do not know for certain their names, but tradition has their names as Balthasar, Melchior, and Gaspar. A treatise, written around 700 AD entitled *Excerpta et Collectanea*, actually offered descriptions of them which imply they are of different ethnicities, with one even being said to have black skin.

The traditional celebration of Epiphany considers all of this and focuses on the wise men because their visit had such spiritual significance. It symbolizes the whole world, represented by men of different ethnicities, coming to see, know, and worship the Savior. Their gifts are also seen as symbolic, with gold representing Christ's royal standing, frankincense his divine birth, and myrrh his death.

In spite of all the things we do not know about the Magi, there are some things we do know which can inspire and encourage us in our walks with the Lord. They were people who, through diligent study, had come to understand God's plan for the ages. They believed His word, sought after Him even though it meant traveling hundreds of miles, eagerly gave Him precious gifts, and worshiped Him when they found Him.

Do we do this? Do we study God's word to better understand Him and His plan for us? Do we freely give what we have to Him like our time, our talents, and even our money? Do we worship Him with our whole beings?

Prayer: Heavenly Father, thank You for moving in the hearts of the Magi, stirring them to seek You. Stir in our hearts too, Lord. And when we seek You, let us find You. In Jesus' name, Amen.

Thought for the Day: Do you have a heart like the Magi?

Day 3: Worship

by Harriet
Read: Psalm 100

Ascribe to the LORD
the glory due his name;
worship the LORD
in the splendor of his holiness.
Psalm 29:2 (NIV)

You sit in your pew on a bright Sunday morning in January. Though the world is cold, your church is warm. The sun streaks through the beautiful stained-glass window, making color splotches on the pew in front of you. The choir rises and bursts into song. Is this worship?

Yes, it is worship, but worship is more than just the songs we sing on Sundays during a church service, the prayers we offer, or the money we place in an offering plate, though all of these can be forms, or acts of worship, if they are done with sincere hearts. They are, in fact, ways in which we show our worship, but worship is much more.

An online dictionary defines worship as honor or homage paid to God or to any deity or object regarded as sacred. The acts listed above—church songs, prayer, financial giving—certainly may honor God, but true worship involves more than just outward acts. It requires a heart that reveres God. A motivation for worship could come from a desire to impress others, for example, or maybe for a tax exemption for charitable giving, rather than from a heart that truly wants to honor God.

The wise men worshiped Jesus when they finally found him. They even gave this as their stated reason for setting out on such a long trek to begin with—they wanted to worship the newborn King. Their worship included offering gifts to Jesus, but as far as we know, it did not include songs. However, David and other psalmists often encouraged singing as part of worship. One such time is found in Psalm 100:2, which says to come before God with joyful songs.

Psalm 100, the reading passage for today, is actually a great place to go to find information on what true worship is all about. That psalm paints a picture of worship. Look at it carefully. What does it include in its picture of worship? It tells us to:

- shout and sing—use our voices to express our worship
- do something for God
- be glad
- know God
- enter into His gates, or in other words, come to His house
- give Him praise and thanksgiving

What does all of this have to do with Epiphany? By one definition, the word epiphany means an appearance or manifestation of something. When we celebrate it on our church calendar, we see it as the first manifestation of Christ to the Gentiles, as symbolized by the visit from the Magi. It was through the Gentiles that Jesus formed His church. Ephesians 2:19-22 gives, perhaps, the best understanding of how followers of Christ, both Jew and Gentile, became His church. It says, "So then you are no longer strangers and aliens, but you are fellow citizens with the saints and members of the household of God, built on the foundation of the apostles and prophets, Christ Jesus himself being the cornerstone, in whom the whole structure, being joined together, grows into a holy temple in the Lord. In Him you also are being built together into a dwelling place for God by the Spirit."

May we, as the people of God woven together by His hand to become His church, worship Him with all our hearts, whether gathered together in corporate worship or in our individual lives!

Prayer: Father, You have made us into Your beloved church. We worship You not because we have to or for selfish reasons, but because You are God, and worthy of our worship. In Jesus' name, Amen.

Thought for the Day: How will you demonstrate your worship of God today?

Day 4: Grafted In

by Harriet
Read: Romans 11:24-29

After this I looked, and there before me
was a great multitude
that no one could count,
from every nation, tribe,
people and language,
standing before the throne
and before the Lamb.
Revelation 7:9 (NIV)

You can blame it on my parents, I suppose. They set the precedent many years ago.

One day, while they were serving as missionaries in Nigeria, a young boy knocked on their door. When Mom answered, there in front of her stood Abel, a bright, smiling Nigerian child about twelve or thirteen years old. He came seeking employment. Back then, Nigerian children were only educated through elementary school. After that, if they could not afford a private education, their school days were over, and they looked for work.

Abel was a precious child. My parents employed him and quickly became extremely fond of him. He proved to be a hard worker and very trustworthy. Every weekday, Abel arrived at our house in the morning and left in the evening. He was just a few years older than my siblings and me and he soon became our constant friend and companion. We loved him very much. He used to tease and tell us he was our brother and even started calling my parents "Mom" and "Dad" too.

Eventually, my mom and dad sent Abel to a private high school in Nigeria, where he received high marks. Later, my parents brought him to America and sent him to college. During this time, he spent all vacations and holidays at our house, still calling my parents "Mom" and "Dad." After college, he married a Nigerian woman who came to the states to marry him. Then they returned to Nigeria, but the situation was dire and eventually they came back to the US.

Today, he and his family are US citizens and a part of my family. They are no different from my other siblings and their children. We see them at every family vacation and holiday, and we have for the past 35 years.

Abel's daughter married a young preacher a few years ago. He's a wonderful young man—kind, intelligent, and also quite Caucasian. They have two beautiful biracial children. Abel's son, likewise, married a Caucasian woman and they, too, now have a biracial child. They are good company to my grandson, who is also biracial.

A couple of years ago, one of my sons and his wife chose to adopt after years of infertility. They worked through a US adoption agency and eagerly waited to see which precious child God would bring to their family. Then the call came. A young mother in the Marshall Islands had selected them to raise her unborn child. Our family was ecstatic as they flew to Hawaii to await the birth of their daughter, Ellie. She is such a treasure!

And somehow, it feels perfect for me, someone born in Africa, who has always felt a little like the description in Hebrews 11—a stranger in a foreign country, searching for a home—to now have a family, both immediate and extended, that consists of people from so many different nations, kindred, and tongues, as Revelation 7 depicts in that beautiful passage of all the people who will gather around God's throne in heaven.

When I read Paul's words in Romans 11:17 about Gentiles being grafted into God's family alongside the Jews, I can relate. I understand the joys of a mixed family with grafted-in members. When we gather for a family reunion, we have in our midst black, brown, blond, red, and gray hair, blue, brown, and green eyes, straight and curly hair. We have round eyes and almond eyes, brown, ruddy, olive, and pale skin, and a joy that is overflowing!

Prayer: Heavenly Father, surely this is what You had in mind when You grafted Gentiles into Your family—people of every tribe, tongue, and nation praising You! May we learn to love those who are different from us as You do. In Jesus' name, Amen.

Thought for the Day: God's skin is multicolored, like His family.

Day 5: The Gospel

by Harriet
Read: John 4:34-38

And they sang a new song, saying:
"You are worthy to take the scroll
and to open its seals,
because you were slain, and with your
blood you purchased
for God persons from every tribe and
language and people and nation."
Revelation 5:9 (NIV)

The gospel is the story of Jesus Christ—His life, death, and resurrection—and the fact that through Him we can find forgiveness of our sins and gain eternal life. Our sin separates us from God, but Jesus paid the penalty for that sin when He died on the cross. Then He conquered death by rising again the third day. Because of His death and subsequent resurrection, we may regain fellowship with God and become children of God through faith alone, in Christ alone. This is sometimes referred to as the good news, and truly, what better news is there than to know that if we accept Jesus as our personal Savior, acknowledging that his death paid the price for our sins, we gain eternal life.

An interesting thing happened in human history a little bit prior to the time of Christ's birth. A couple of hundred years before Jesus was born, Alexander the Great, considered by some to be the greatest military leader of all time, conquered what was known of the world at that time. Under his rule, he made Greek the common language for all his people, requiring them to learn it instead of the language they had been using. He died suddenly at only thirty-three years of age from an unknown cause; perhaps an illness or possibly even poisoning. His empire outlived him, but in time it was progressively absorbed into the ever-spreading Roman Empire.

The Roman Empire was known for many things, including its infrastructure. The Romans built a complex system of roads that were vital to the maintenance and development of the empire. These roads provided a means for overland movement of armies, officials, and civilians. But these wonderful roads also provided a means of fast, efficient travel for something else—the gospel!

So, amazingly, when the Gospels were written, the good news of salvation traveled fast along this complex, efficient road system built by the Romans. And as it traveled, it could be read by all of the literate people in the known world at that time, because it was written in Greek and by then, all literate people read Greek. Isn't God good! His timing is always perfect!

The Bible tells us that the gospel came first to the Jews. Then the Gentiles were grafted into God's family by means of salvation in Christ through the hearing of the gospel. This astonishing work of God is also a part of what we celebrate during Epiphany.

What does the gospel mean to you? Do you understand your need for a solution to your sin problem? Have you acknowledged Christ's sacrifice for your sins and prayed to accept Him as your Savior? If not, you can do that right now. If you have, what are you doing to share the gospel with others so that they too can have their sins forgiven and be grafted into God's family?

Prayer: Heavenly Father, Your word clearly tells us about Your plan of salvation to those who will believe it. Help us to eagerly share this with others who have not believed. In Jesus' name, Amen.

Thought for the Day: "For God so loved the world that he gave his one and only Son, that whoever believes in him shall not perish but have eternal life" (John 3:16 NIV).

Chapter 4

Winter Hymns

Day 1: God's Holiness:
A Proper Response
by Shirley
Read: Isaiah 6:1-6

And one called to another and said:
"Holy, holy, holy is the LORD of hosts;
the whole earth is full of his glory!"
Isaiah 6:3

For as long as I can remember, I have been fascinated by the pomp, ceremony, and tradition surrounding British royalty. I grew up hearing stories of Queen Elizabeth II's 1956 visit to Nigeria (I was not born yet) from my parents, siblings, and missionary aunts, uncles, and cousins. These stories are so familiar that they seem to be a part of my memories of witnessing the actual events, instead of merely stories I have heard.

Granted, the pomp and ceremony looked much different in Nigeria than it did in Great Britain, yet it was a time to get the cities cleaned and spiffed up, have everyone dressed in their finest clothing, highlight the culture of Nigeria, and for everyone to behave well and use their best manners.

There are all sorts of traditional protocols concerning how you relate to the Queen of England and other monarchs. The idea that a king or queen should be treated with deference comes from a biblical, historical understanding that they are chosen by God. It sounds like these folks, at least in the beginning, understood Romans 13:1. "For there is no authority except from God, and those that exist have been instituted by God."

Many free-spirited Americans mock the protocol and rules of British royalty, yet Americans have our own rules of protocol when meeting our US President. And if you are a Southerner, from the time you are a tiny tyke, rules of protocol (or etiquette) are drilled into you for how you interact with other people. That's right, isn't it?

"Yes, ma'am."

It is with these images of royal, presidential, and southern protocol in mind that we look at today's key passage that begins talking about King Uzziah. A read through 2 Chronicles 26 tells us about this king of Israel. He was a good king for most of his reign, but toward the end of his rule, his pride grew out of control resulting in his being afflicted with leprosy and his eventual death, bringing his 52-year reign to a shameful end. The people of Israel were left feeling their future would be bleak. They were without hope.

There, in the midst of the uncertainty and confusion Israel was experiencing, Isaiah looked up and saw a glorious sight—God sitting on His throne reigning as the absolute Sovereign God of the Universe. This was reassuring to Isaiah, and through him, to the Israelites and to us. Regardless of how bleak things seem, and whether or not an earthly king is seated on his throne, God is always on His throne! He was, is, and evermore shall be the living God. One symbol of a king's status is his clothing. Here, the train of God's robe filled the entire temple, signifying His magnificence.

Isaiah is allowing us to look over his shoulder at the vision by pulling aside a curtain to allow us a peek into the throne room of the King of kings. The seraphim (magnificent, powerful creatures) were flying above the throne.

Remember the protocols for interacting with

royalty? The seraphim teach us the protocols for how we interact with the King, God—holy and sovereign—The Holy One of Israel (Isaiah 45:11).

God is so holy, so powerful, so magnificent, that His presence engenders a profound sense of awe, reverence, and respect as we see in the actions of the seraphim in the throne room. Everything the seraphim do shows humble submission to and respect for the Sovereign God of the Universe. A handwritten note in my Bible says, "seraphim show us how impure beings offer homage to God's divine holiness."

What protocols for interacting with God do we learn from the seraphim's actions? We are to approach God with an intense reverence as we acknowledge our unworthiness to behold His glory. This reminds us that in our sinful state we cannot clearly see God. We are to approach God fully aware of our sin and imperfections as we walk through our lives. We are to always be ready and quick to actively serve God and proclaim the gospel of Christ.

Isaiah's vision destroys our incorrect view of how we are to approach God. It reminds us that God is so holy and great that we cannot approach Him except through the shed blood of His Son, Jesus.

Reginald Heber wrote the words to the majestic hymn, "Holy, Holy, Holy! Lord God Almighty," that echoes our passage as each verse begins with "Holy, holy, holy!" The third verse is:

> Holy, holy, holy! Lord God Almighty!
> All Thy works shall praise Thy Name,
> in earth, and sky, and sea;
> Holy, holy, holy; merciful and mighty!
> God in three Persons, blessed Trinity!

Prayer: Holy God, forgive us for the casual and often lazy way we approach You. Show us Your holiness. Thank You for making a way for us— sinful as we are—to approach You and have a personal relationship with You through the shed blood of Your Son, Jesus, in whose name we pray, Amen.

Thought for the Day: How has God's holiness shaken you? Tony Reinke says, "The tremors of God's holiness shake us to the core."

Day 2: Pointing to God's Almighty Throne

by Shirley
Read: Psalm 8

For since the creation of the world
God's invisible qualities
—his eternal power and divine nature—
have been clearly seen, being understood
from what has been made,
so that people are without excuse.
Romans 1:20 (NIV)

God's masterpieces in creation continually amaze me. Think about the massiveness of the Grand Canyon, the brilliance of the setting sun, and a phenomenally colored rainbow. Also consider God's intricate creation, man. Our physical bodies, comprised of cells, tissues, and organs, are absolutely remarkable (Psalm 139:14). In man, we also see a spiritual masterpiece as we are redeemed (Ephesians 1:7) and saved by God's grace (Ephesians 2:8).

These are just a few examples of God's

masterpieces that give persuasive testimony—through their majesty, awe, beauty, and grace—to the power and eternality of God who sits on His throne in heaven and sustains all that He created.

God, in Job 37:14, tells Job, "Hear this, O Job; stop and consider the wondrous works of God." Continuing through chapter 39, God tells Job all the things He does in creation. Job's reply to God is "The Almighty ... he is great in power" (Job 37:23).

Creation so loudly proclaims the existence of Creator God that there is no excuse for not believing in Him (Romans 1:19-20). Commentator Matthew Henry said about creation, "The variety, multitude, order ... do abundantly prove a Creator and his eternal power and Godhead ... Thus did the light shine in the darkness. And this from the creation of the world. Though some have greater light and means of knowledge than others, yet all have enough to leave them inexcusable."

A lesser-known hymn, "The Voices of Creation," written by Valdimar Briem, beautifully describes the ways creation shows the glory of God. The second verse shows how the mountains distinctly reveal Him: "The snow-capped peaks are pointing to God's almighty throne." Verse three reminds us that God is in control:

> The ocean's vast abysses in one grand
>   psalm record,
> The deep mysterious counsels and mercies
>   of the Lord;
> The icy waves of winter are thund'ring on
>   the strand;
> And grief's chill stream is guided by
>   God's all-gracious hand.

The other verses tell us how all of nature proclaims God's majesty, and the hosts of stars sing "of God's majestic temple and palace courts on high."

Psalm 11:4 tells us, "The LORD is in his holy temple; the LORD's throne is in heaven." Matthew 6:9 tells us, "Pray then like this: "Our Father in heaven, hallowed be your name." John Calvin's comment on this verse says that to speak of God being in heaven "separates him from the rank of creatures, and reminds us that, when we think of him, we ought not to form any low or earthly conceptions: for he is higher than the whole world."

Isaiah gives us a glimpse into the throne room of God where He is seated. He is so holy, powerful, and magnificent that a profound sense of awe, reverence, and respect results in praise and adoration for who He is.

The prophet Habakkuk comes to my mind here. As in the Job passage that we looked at earlier, Habakkuk had a long conversation with God in Habakkuk chapters 1, 2, and 3. A handwritten note in the margin of my Bible beside Habakkuk 2:4 reads, "Habakkuk is about sinful (prideful) people being humbled and the righteous living by faith." Habakkuk asks God why He isn't giving justice— what Habakkuk thinks they deserve—to the idol worshipers.

God tells Habakkuk all the things that He controls. In response to God's words, Habakkuk says, "I hear and my body trembles.... Yet I will quietly wait ..." (Habakkuk 3:16). He continues, saying regardless of the hardships that come, "I will take joy in the God of my salvation. God, the Lord is my strength, he makes my feet like the deer's, and he makes me tread on my high places" (Habakkuk 3:19).

God reminds us through Scripture and scriptural hymns that "the LORD is in His holy temple" (Habakkuk 2:20), unlike the useless, lifeless idols evil ones are worshiping. It is important here to remember Scripture also says that God is omnipresent (everywhere at the same time), so His being on His almighty throne in heaven does not mean He just sits on that throne unaware of all that is happening on earth and with us. In Jeremiah, we read, "'Can a man hide himself in secret places so that I cannot see him?' declares the LORD. 'Do I not fill heaven and earth?' declares the LORD" (Jeremiah 23:24).

Our doxology for today is from Joseph Haydn's "The Heavens are Telling the Glory of God."

The heavens are telling the glory of God,
The wonder of His work displays the firmament.

And all God's people said, *Ti ti lailai, Amin!*

This is a Yoruba (Nigerian language) phrase meaning, "Forever and ever, amen!"

Prayer: Almighty God, we thank You for the intricacy and beauty of the world. Help us recognize all the ways creation points to You and respond in grateful praise and adoration. In Jesus' name, Amen.

Thought for the Day: Everything in creation points to God's almighty throne and the God who sustains life and creation. Throughout the day, identify aspects of creation that point to God.

Day 3: 'Tis Winter Now

by Shirley
Read: Psalm 147:12-18

God thunders wondrously with his voice;
he does great things
that we cannot comprehend.
By the breath of God ice is given, and the
broad waters are frozen fast.
Job 37:5, 10

About a year before my mom's death, a sweet lady moved into the apartment next to us. The day she was moving in it was freezing cold. Her apartment had been empty for a while, and the heat had not been turned on in advance of her arrival. Mom was concerned the lady would get too cold, so she sent me over to invite her to come to our apartment and have a cup of coffee and visit while everything got moved in.

I introduced myself, and she said, "Call me Mimi, everyone does." She was grateful for the offer and Mom, Mimi, and I had a great visit.

About a week later, Mom, Mimi, and I met a couple of other friends for supper. Everyone was talking about how cold and dreary it was. Different ones were talking about their aches and pains. Mimi was very quiet. After a little while, I said, "Mimi, how do you handle the cold?"

I need to break into my story to tell you, I was used to Mom singing answers to my questions, but I had never known anyone else who did—until that moment!

Mimi answered, slightly changing the words, by singing: "God warmly in His love enfolds and keeps me through life's wintry days." Guess what? Mom knew that hymn and started singing with her.

> 'Tis winter now; the fallen snow
> Has left the heavens all coldly clear;
> Through leafless boughs the sharp winds
> blow,
> And all the earth lies dead and drear.

I didn't know this hymn written by Samuel Longfellow, "'Tis Winter Now, the Fallen Snow," so I had to look it up when I got home. Isn't this verse a perfect description of winter? Cold, leafless boughs, sharp winds, earth lying dead and drear.

In the same way, there are times when things in our lives get hectic and we are tired of the day-to-day drudgery of life and the continual barrage of trials. We are prone to have pity parties and feel sorry for ourselves as we focus on what we don't have or how many bad things are occurring around us.

The second verse paints a beautiful and comforting picture of God.

> And yet God's love is not withdrawn;
> His life within the keen air breathes;
> His beauty paints the crimson dawn,
> And clothes each branch with glittering
>   wreaths.

God cares for His creation and does not withdraw His love. Can't you see in your mind's eye the beautiful winter sunrises?

During our days of drudgery and trials, it is important for us to remember that God loves us and is present with us all the time. He takes care of us.

This is precisely what Mimi was saying when I asked her about the cold weather. She wasn't ignoring the reality of the cold, the joint pain she experienced, or the need to stay warm, she was simply testifying to God's faithfulness to keep her, and us, in His warm love and care.

Her answer came from the third verse:

O God, you give the winter's cold,
As well as summer's joyous rays,
You warmly in your love enfold,
And keep us through life's wintry days.

This verse acknowledges that the seasons in creation and our spiritual lives are in God's control, and reminds us that in life's winter season, God warmly enfolds us in His love, and keeps His children safe and warm.

What a magnificent truth from the Bible. God is faithful to those who are His children. We place our hope and confidence in the fact that God will do what He promised those whom He has redeemed. 1 Corinthians 1:8-9 says, "He will also keep you firm to the end, so that you will be blameless on the day of our Lord Jesus Christ. God is faithful, who has called you into fellowship with His Son, Jesus Christ our Lord."

Our responsibility in those winter seasons is to look to Jesus for our strength and to trust He will protect us, regardless of the season in which we find ourselves.

Psalm 121:1-2 (NIV) reinforces this, "I lift up my eyes to the mountains—where does my help come from? My help comes from the Lord, the Maker of heaven and earth."

Prayer: Our gracious Heavenly Father, it is sometimes hard for us to trust You when the drudgery of life and the barrage of trials hit. Help us understand You more so that we will trust You more. Thank You for enfolding us in the warmth of Your love. In Jesus' name, Amen.

Thought for the Day: Rest securely in the warmth of God's love that keeps "us through life's wintry days."

Day 4: Trusting Jesus

by Shirley
Read: Ephesians 5:1-13

Trust in the LORD with all your heart,
And lean not on your own understanding;
In all your ways acknowledge Him,
And He will make straight your paths.
Proverbs 3:5-6

Numerous women whom I have counseled through the years have struggled so much with all the things they dealt with in their day-to-day lives and the trials that seemed to knock the breath out of them and leave them defeated.

Some of those struggles have been the result of unconfessed sin. But so many of the struggles concerned how to make godly and wise decisions. Their struggles often stemmed from their lack of understanding of what it means to be a Christ-follower. Many come to a saving knowledge of Christ and everyone is so excited that they have become Christ-followers, but sadly, many new

Christ-followers are not discipled—taught what Scripture says and how to apply that Scripture to real life.

That lack of discipling, which I prefer to call disciple-making, often leaves Christ-followers defeated. They do not have the biblical knowledge, understanding, and equipping they need so they know they can have absolute trust in God.

Christ-followers have a command from God and a responsibility to make disciple-makers. By this I mean, to make disciples who in turn make disciples, who in turn make disciples, and so on.

I remember a decision that Mom and I needed to make immediately following the death of my brother Tim—whether or not to move from the home where the three of us had lived. We sat down one morning after breakfast and made our list of pros and cons. The pros to move forward with what we were thinking far outweighed the cons.

Now that we had convinced ourselves, in writing, that we needed to move, the next question was, where?

We each scoured the listings for homes and apartments for rent. With each one I saw, I proclaimed it too small, too far away, too expensive, not in a safe neighborhood, and so on.

Before long, Mom starting singing,

Simply trusting every day,
Trusting through a stormy way;
Even when my faith is small,
Trusting Jesus, that is all.

Do you know "Trusting Jesus," a great hymn of faith by Edgar P. Stites?

I would like to tell you that my initial reaction to Mom's singing was to roll my eyes and say, "Come on, Mom. That doesn't help." And yes, I did—and do—know better than that!

Mom replied by singing a verse of another great hymn, "Trust and Obey," by John H. Sammis:

Not a burden we bear,
Not a sorrow we share,
But our toil He doth richly repay;
Not a grief nor a loss,
Nor a frown nor a cross,
But is blest if we trust and obey.

Mom was right as she responded with these hymns, wasn't she? All we had to do was trust Jesus. It couldn't really be that simple, could it?

The answer, of course, is a resounding, "Absolutely!"

So, how exactly do we do that? How do we learn to trust Jesus? We learn to trust Jesus as we come to know Him better through His Holy Spirit-inspired Bible and through spending time with Him in prayer. Add to that, a Christ-follower walking alongside us in a disciple-making relationship that shows us how to live our lives in a manner that pleases God—obeying His commands.

Since God is sovereign, faithful, and loving, we can trust Him in every situation. He will lead and protect us, all the while giving us the wisdom and discernment needed to make wise choices and decisions. God is 100% sovereign and we are 100% responsible.

Today's passage reaffirms that truth, "Walk as children of light (for the fruit of light is found in all that is good and right and true) and try to discern what is pleasing to the Lord" (Ephesians 5:8b-10).

Prayer: Heavenly Father, forgive us for the times we fail to trust You. Help us know how to make disciple-makers who know how to trust You. Thank You that You do not leave us alone to figure out how to walk throughout our day. In Jesus' name, Amen.

Thought for the Day: "Brightly does His Spirit shine into this poor heart of mine; While He leads, I cannot fall; Trusting Jesus, that is all." –verse two of "Trusting Jesus."

Day 5: Sun of My Soul

by Shirley
Read: Psalm 84:8-12

For the LORD God is a sun and shield;
The LORD will give grace and glory;
No good thing will He withhold
From those who walk uprightly.
Psalm 84:11 (NKJV)

I am not a huge fan of camping for numerous reasons. A group of my friends finally convinced me to go on a weekend camping trip with them. Since it was in early winter, we (mostly they) made sure we had all the necessary equipment to keep us warm.

Several hours before we were to set out on what I was calling our wilderness adventure, the two most experienced campers let us know that they would have to meet us at the campsite several hours later than the rest of us would arrive.

Later on that afternoon, the other six of us hiked—okay, we really walked leisurely—a little way to the campsite and began getting the tents set up and a fire built and started before nightfall. While the campfire provided light as the darkness settled upon us, we also had several large lanterns that provided a good deal of bright light.

We were talking and laughing and having a great time. One of the guys had recorded a 120-minute cassette tape of another friend of ours playing the piano, which I was excited to hear. The tape was a great mix of hymns, classical, and contemporary (this was in the 80s) music. All six of us were music lovers so we listened intently, paying little attention to anything else going on around us.

I noticed three of our group get up to retrieve blankets from their tents, but that didn't really register with me because I was so engrossed in listening to a magnificent performance of Rachmaninoff's "Rhapsody on a Theme of Paganini, Variation 18."

When the cassette tape ended, we suddenly were aware that the fire had gone out—the lantern light kept us from noticing. I suddenly realized that I was so cold I was shivering. Now for those of you who don't know me, I rarely get cold. My being so cold was a bit unsettling to me.

About that time the two most experienced campers appeared and got a roaring fire going and saved us from freezing to death. (That might be a slight exaggeration.)

Isn't what happened that evening on the camping trip exactly what happens to us in our spiritual lives? As Christ-followers we have been redeemed by the shed blood of Jesus Christ, our Savior.

We make preparations for our spiritual journey as we carefully ensure that we guard our relationship with Christ. We read, study, memorize, meditate and contemplate upon Scripture. We spend time in prayer, listen and learn from biblically sound teaching and preaching, and enjoy fellowship with our brothers and sisters in Christ.

We set up our surroundings as we place ourselves under the spiritual authority of those whom God has placed in authority over us. We live in community with those in our local church in such a way that we encourage, support, admonish, and hold each other accountable to live our lives in a way that glorifies God.

We begin to depend so much on the lanterns—works—that we do not realize the fire has dimmed or gone out. We get so involved with all the things occurring in our lives and the lives of those around us, we become distracted. We do not realize we are going through the motions of following Christ, not experiencing the real warmth and light He provides. Our passion to know Him and experience His mercy, grace, kindness, love, and warmth has dimmed. That passion is sometimes squelched because of unconfessed sin.

John Keble wrote the hymn, "Sun of My Soul," from the biblical foundation of today's passage. This hymn reminds us of God's everlasting love and the light His presence brings in every moment of our lives.

> Sun of my soul, Thou Savior dear,
> It is not night if Thou be near;
> Oh, may no earthborn cloud arise
> To hide Thee from Thy servant's eyes.

Don't you love this reminder? God is indeed the sun, the light, of our souls. When God is our

Savior, His light brightens and warms us, even when the darkness of life looms around us. The light of His presence guides us through the darkness.

The second verse speaks to us as we wander away from God. The last two lines are a prayer, "Lord, the gracious work begin; Let him (the sinner) no more lie down in sin."

What a glorious reminder that God's gracious work will bring forgiveness and restoration to us when we have sinned. Our responsibility is to confess that sin and ask His forgiveness, and then walk in His gracious warmth.

Prayer: Gracious Heavenly Father, thank You for always being with us, the warmth of Your love, and Your light that leads us through the darkness. In Jesus' name, Amen.

Thought for the Day: The light of God's presence and the warmth of His love will sustain us every step of our journey.

Harriet E. Michael   Shirley Crowder

Chapter 5

Let it Snow!

Day 1: The Excellency of Our God

by Shirley
Read: Isaiah 35:1-2

But we have this treasure in earthen
vessels, that the excellency
of the power may be of God, and not of us.
2 Corinthians 4:7 (KJV)

A dear senior saint at the church where I work diligently keeps the roses blooming in the garden at the side of the front entrance. I pass by and see these beauties every time I enter and exit the building. What beautiful reminders of God's creation! I often clip one for my desk and enjoy its beauty and fragrance for several days.

I remember seeing pictures of snow when I was a child in Nigeria and hearing my mom, dad, and other missionaries talk about snow. But when we returned to the States, to Alabama, snow was infrequent. Winters in Central Alabama tend to bring a lot of rain, and often only cool temperatures.

A substantial snow—by Alabama standards—

blanketed the Birmingham area one winter. That morning, while there were icy road issues in some places, the snow was powdery white and beautiful as it covered everything.

As I walked past the rose garden that morning to enter the building, much to my delight, I saw a magnificent deep pink rose that seemingly broke through the coldness of the layer of snow.

The starkness of the white against the rose magnified the richness of its deep pink color as if proclaiming the resplendent glory and strength of its Creator God. I was reminded of a prophecy about the coming of Jesus Christ, "Then a shoot will spring from the stem of Jesse" (Isaiah 11:1a NASB).

I have heard that the rose is considered the most perfect of all flowers. So, since Jesus is absolutely perfect in every way, He is often referred to as a rose. Isaiah 35:1-2 comes to mind:

> The wilderness and the wasteland shall be
>   glad for them,
> And the desert shall rejoice and blossom as
>   the rose;

It shall blossom abundantly and rejoice,
Even with joy and singing …
They shall see the glory of the Lord,
The excellency of our God.

While the snow in Birmingham covered things and made everything look pure white and clean, the dirt was just covered up. That's what we try to do sometimes, isn't it? We try to clean up or cover up our sin, and we fail miserably. The good news for Christ-followers is that Jesus Christ took our sin and the wrath we deserve upon Himself.

As I closely examined that rose, I could see the dirt on the ground showing through the breaks in the snow, and numerous thoughts flooded my mind.

To me, that rose, although a deep pink, represented the shed blood of Christ, through which we have been saved from our sin and our various futile attempts to get ourselves cleaned up.

The green stem reminded me of the "stem of Jesse" (Isaiah 11:1), which points to Jesus coming to earth and living as fully God and fully man. I've heard it said that leaves represent God's truth, which is the Holy Spirit-inspired Bible that makes us a new creation and gives us new life in Christ!

A wonderful old hymn by Robert Lowry comes to mind: "Nothing But the Blood of Jesus:"

What can wash away my sin?
    Nothing but the blood of Jesus;
What can make me whole again?
    Nothing but the blood of Jesus.
Oh! precious is the flow
    That makes me white as snow;
No other fount I know,
    Nothing but the blood of Jesus.

I wrote a note in the margin of my Bible next to Isaiah 35 that says, "God's nature and character are His excellence, perfection, and glory."

We see the excellency of God shine in His attributes: holiness, greatness, goodness, love, justice, truthfulness, and wisdom. And I saw the excellency of God shine in a magnificent deep pink rose breaking through the coldness of the snow.

Prayer: Gracious Heavenly Father, give us a passion to know You better so that we will trust

You more as we recognize and gain a deeper understanding of the excellency of Your holiness, greatness, goodness, love, justice, truthfulness, and wisdom. In Jesus' name, Amen.

Thought for the Day: The excellency of God shines in and through His creation. Do you recognize God's excellency in creation?

Day 2: There's No Place Like Home

by Harriet
Read: Hebrews 11:9-10, 13-16

... they desired a better country,
that is a heavenly one.
Therefore God is not ashamed
to be called their God.
Hebrews 11:16 (NASB)

The forecast called for snow, snow, and more snow! My husband was out of town, so I called him and told him what was coming our way. He cut his trip short and headed back home. Sure enough, the snow came down as predicted. By the time he pulled in our driveway, it was already coming down hard, and it didn't stop snowing for two days! When it finally stopped, we had thirteen inches of the white stuff on the ground. Schools canceled classes; businesses closed, and only emergency services stayed open.

This was back when the only thing available to melt snow off the roads was salt. My family was snowed in for days! Fortunately, I had paid attention to the forecast and purchased enough food and milk for a week. And though many in our city lost electricity, we were fortunate in that our electricity stayed on.

We spent that week at home. My children loved it! Each day we all slept late, the children played in the snow, and I was still able to wash their wet clothes and feed them warm dinners each evening since our electricity stayed on. We had a small evergreen tree in our front yard—a pine with prickly needles. It was so thoroughly covered with snow that my children climbed up it as if climbing a mountain.

That big snow that shut down my southern city was many years ago. My children are grown now and the pine tree in our yard is huge. But I still recall it as one of the most pleasant weeks of my life because I and mine were safe at home and had all of our needs met.

We all have the instinctive desire and longing for home. Hebrews 11 talks of men and women of faith who longed for a better home—one that is built by God Himself. Verse 16 amazes me. It says of these people, that God was not ashamed to be called their God. What does it take for it to please God to be called your God? Do you have to do some mighty deed or achieve a high level of spirituality? No, you simply have to have a longing for a better place—a heavenly place, a city whose architect and builder is God!

I can relate to these verses because, though I love my home in America, there is a restlessness in my spirit when I think of home. I am a Third Culture Kid, often referred to as a TCK. Shirley is one too. TCKs are people, children and adults, who were born and reared in a country that is not the country of their citizenship. This group of people, which include the children of foreign missionaries, like Shirley and me, have some common traits. One of them is an ambiguity as to where home is, and a constant yearning for a place where they no longer live.

As Christians, we are all TCKs in a way. We are all living in a place that is not really our home. Our home is a better place—a heavenly place, a city whose architect and builder is God!

Prayer: Heavenly Father, You have placed deep in our hearts a longing for home. Help us to realize this is because You are preparing a home for us. Help us to understand that we are truly strangers on this earth making our way to the city whose builder is You. In Your Son's name, Amen.

Thought for the Day: There's no place like home. For believers, home is wherever God places us until He eventually calls us to Himself in our eternal home.

Day 3: Is Your Faith Melting?

by Shirley
Read: Hebrews 10:32-39

*But we are not of those who shrink back
and are destroyed,
but of those who have faith
and preserve their souls.*
Hebrews 10:39

Many years ago, we experienced one of those rare events in Alabama, a covering of beautiful powdery snow fell overnight blanketing everything. It was so pristine and white that the sun reflecting off it was both glorious and blinding.

I bundled up and headed out for a walk. My footprints were the first to break through and crush down the snow in a field behind my apartment. I found a large fallen tree limb where I could sit and soak in the beautiful scenery. Soon, snowballs and birds flew, and dogs and children ran, jumped, and played.

I decided to go check on several of my elderly

friends in a nearby neighborhood. A few hours later I returned to my spot on the fallen tree limb to find a much different scene. The sun had come out, making it a good deal warmer. That, plus the trampling of feet—dogs, children, and adults—had turned that beautiful snow-covered wonderland into a wet and muddy mess!

My thoughts made a correlation between snow and faith. Once we become Christ-followers, the Holy Spirit increases our faith so we can overcome the trials, struggles, and unbelief that Paul reminds us will come our way.

At the start, we are excited to be following Jesus and want to tell everyone about Him and how He saved us. As we come to know more about God, our faith begins to grow. Other Christ-followers come alongside us to teach, encourage, and admonish us.

Then life gets busy and our schedules fill. The struggles of living in a fallen world hit us one after another, often at the same time. We stop reading and studying the Bible and praying, we are not careful in what we choose to read or watch, and we make unwise or sinful choices about what we do.

We become disheartened and tired.

Suddenly—it has actually been gradually, but it takes a while to notice it—we realize our faith has been melting away. How do we revive our faith? Hebrews 10:35-36 gives us a hint: "Therefore do not throw away your confidence, which has a great reward." We are to continue trusting God and having confidence the Bible is true even though we don't *feel* like it is true. The writer of Hebrews continues in verse 36, "For you have need of endurance ..."

We read, "Therefore lift your drooping hands and strengthen your weak knees, and make straight paths for your feet, so that what is lame may not be put out of joint but rather be healed" (Hebrews 12:12-13). When we are in a spiritual winter we certainly need to rest, but we also need to be disciplined in exercising our faith so it will grow strong again.

As I was studying and contemplating melting faith, I remembered a book I read: *Habits of Grace* by David Mathis. Mathis writes about spiritual disciplines, something many of us lack in our lives. He outlines three main spiritual disciplines that are valuable in the lives of every Christ-follower. He outlines biblical truth and how to apply it to our lives. Using his headings, we'll answer the question asked earlier, "How do we revive our faith?"

"Hear His Voice (Word)" – We must be consistently diligent to put aside time to be in the Bible. We must read, study, memorize, meditate, and contemplate upon it at least daily. This is how our thinking can "be transformed" and our faith strengthened (Romans 12:2).

"Have His Ear (Prayer)" – We must learn to pray, not just the rote "God help me" prayers, although these are certainly appropriate and needed at times. As we come to know God better through His Holy-Spirit-inspired Bible, we will learn to trust Him more, which results in our being bolder in our prayers. The deeper our communication with God, the stronger our faith.

"Belong to His Body (Fellowship)" – We must belong to a local church as we submit ourselves to the leadership and serve God through His church. Sadly, in our culture, many people are looking for what a church can do for them, not how they can serve the Lord in and through the church. Your faith grows stronger as your church family walks alongside you to encourage and admonish you when your faith is melting.

In Isaiah 46:3-5 God tells the people "I will carry you." While that was a promise to a specific people at a specific time, when we look at the whole of Scripture we know that God has carried us in the past, is carrying us now, and will continue carrying us in the future—even when our faith is melting.

Prayer: Gracious Heavenly Father, when our faith is melting, enable us to hold on to the truths we know about You. Bring into our lives Christ-following sisters and brothers to walk beside, encourage, and admonish us. Renew and strengthen our faith. In Jesus' name, Amen.

Thought for the Day: God is our source of strength always and will enable us to persevere until our faith is strong again.

Day 4: Faith

by Harriet
Read: Hebrews 11:1-6

*And without faith
it is impossible to please God,
because anyone who comes to him
must believe that he exists and that he
rewards those who earnestly seek him.*
Hebrews 11:6 (NIV)

I once heard a story about a man who visited a friend in one of the cold, northern states during the wintertime. He and his friend took a walk out in the beautiful snow-covered countryside. Soon they came upon a frozen lake. Thinking they would cross it, they first wanted to make sure the ice would not break under their weight. To be sure it was safe, the man's friend, a resident of this cold state, took a cautious step onto the ice. Then he got down on his hands and knees and slowly began to move forward, firmly hitting each piece of ice ahead of him to make sure it was solid before he inched any farther.

About that time, the man who was gingerly walking in the back heard a noise coming from behind him. Astonished, he turned away from watching his friend, to see what was causing the noise. A hill directly behind him was blocking his view, but in a few seconds, he saw the source of the noise. To his amazement, he saw a horse-drawn sleigh full of people coming toward the frozen lake. This sleigh bounded down the hill and onto the frozen lake alongside of him with reckless abandon, the people waving and laughing as they passed by.

That is a great illustration of faith. It is being absolutely convinced of a different reality, the complete assurance of what one cannot see. This is exactly how the Bible defines faith in today's passage. It is the assurance of things hoped for, the conviction of things not seen. Our key verse reminds us that without faith it is impossible to please God. God wants us to be absolutely convinced of His reality and completely assured of His presence.

Sometimes the challenges that we face seem overwhelming. I have faced times like that and during those times, I have always found it helpful to remember how God has pulled me through before. I remember studying the book of Habakkuk in a Bible study a few years ago. Habakkuk did this. He was very concerned about a situation and called out to God in prayer. Then in Habakkuk 3:3-15, he recalls the many times and ways God had helped him in the past and he concludes that since God worked in the past, He can be trusted with the future.

I do not know why the sleigh full of people came barreling down onto the frozen lake without making sure it would hold. Perhaps they were careless and fortunate to not fall through thin ice. But I think probably they were like Habakkuk. They had most likely been down that path before and knew the ice would hold.

What are you hoping for but not seeing today? Are there some areas in your life where you need to exercise more faith, believing that God will take care of them? Where is God developing more faith in your life? How has He proven faithful in the past?

Prayer: Heavenly Father, strengthen our faith today. Assure us of Your presence and convince us of Your plans. Remind us of how You have helped us in the past. Add more faith to the little faith we have. In Your Son's name, Amen.

Thought for the Day: We never know what the day will bring us. Let's please God with our faith today, regardless of what comes our way.

Day 5: Whiter Than Snow

by Shirley
Read: Psalm 51

Purge me with hyssop,
and I shall be clean;
wash me, and I shall be whiter than snow.
Psalm 51:7

A story about summer may help warm you a bit. On what seemed to be the hottest and most humid day on record, I helped some friends move into their new home. The first phase of that day's move was loading everything from the storage unit into a truck. Once that was done, we went to the new home to unload. It seemed to take forever to unload that truck. Things easily picked up and carried from the storage unit to the truck felt as if they had quadrupled in weight and difficulty. We finally got everything into the house, with at least the furniture in place. I borrowed a beach towel to cover the seat in my friend's car before I got in, so my filth and sweat didn't permeate the seat.

When I arrived home, I headed straight for the shower. As I turned on the light, I caught sight of myself. It was not a pretty picture at all! Sweat and dirt had mixed to form a yucky pasty mud on my neck and face. My hair was soaked with sweat and sticking to my head. As I peeled off my clothing, I had to hold my breath because it was so stinky. I was so tired that I could barely move.

I turned on the cool water and stepped into the shower. I scrubbed and scrubbed to remove all the dirt and sweat, and it took two shampoos to get my hair clean.

Ahh! I exited the bathroom clean and sweet-smelling, and refreshed and reinvigorated. Afterward, I saw a very different person in the mirror—and a better smelling one, too! As wonderful as that shower was and as great as it felt to be clean and refreshed, that was nothing compared to the deep joy of undergoing God's cleansing of our sin.

God promised a day when He would completely cleanse and purify us. "I will sprinkle clean water on you, and you shall be clean from all your uncleannesses, and from all your idols I will cleanse you. And I will give you a new heart, and a new spirit I will put within you. And I will remove the heart of stone from your flesh and give you a heart of flesh" (Ezekiel 36:25-26).

Our sin is so great! Even those sins we think of as *little* sins are grievous offenses to Holy God. Our sin stains our hearts as it puts a wall of separation between us and God. Only God can forgive our sin and erase the guilt and shame we experience because of our sin. "Though your sins are like scarlet, they shall be as white as snow, though they are red like crimson, they shall become like wool" (Isaiah 1:18b).

Our thoughts and attitudes are often sinful. Instead of allowing the Holy Spirit-inspired word of God to transform our thoughts and attitudes (Romans 12:2), we rehearse the same thoughts over and over and justify our sinful attitudes. Only through the power of God can our thoughts and attitudes change. Titus says it this way, "He saved us, not because of works done by us in righteousness, but according to his own mercy, by the washing of regeneration and renewal of the

Holy Spirit" (3:5).

Sin is not the result of an external force; it originates in our hearts (Mark 7:21a). That is why King David prayed, "Create in me a clean heart, O God, and renew a right spirit within me" (Psalm 51:10).

Today's passage is the prayer of confession King David prayed after the prophet Nathan confronted him about his sin with Bathsheba. It is a wonderful example of how to humbly confess sin and ask for God's mercy, grace, and forgiveness.

James Nicholson wrote a wonderful hymn of prayer, "Whiter Than Snow." The verses implore the Lord to make us perfectly whole, holy—a suitable sacrifice—and to create a new heart for us. The sixth verse (you'll have to look it up online since most hymnals do not contain all the verses) is a wonderful statement of faith in God's cleansing power:

> The blessing by faith, I receive from
> above;
> Oh, glory! My soul is made perfect in
> love;

My prayer has prevailed, and this moment
  I know,
The blood is applied, I am whiter than
  snow.

Amen!

Prayer: Gracious Heavenly Father, wash me so that I will be whiter than snow. In Jesus' name, Amen.

Thought for the Day: The precious blood of Christ washes away all of our sin so that we become whiter than the whitest snow.

Chapter 6

Home and Hearth

Day 1: A Child's Heart

by Harriet
Read: Ephesians 6:1-4

My son, give me your heart ...
Proverbs 23:26 (NIV)

Parenting a child can sometimes seem like an almost overwhelming task. Christian parents look to God for help. We search the Scriptures for parenting guidelines, and as we do, we naturally focus on verses in both the Old Testament and the New Testament that emphasize the need for our children to honor and obey us. In fact, in Exodus 20:12, the commandment to honor your father and mother is listed among the Ten Commandments. The biblical requirements for children to honor and obey are clear, appropriate, and right. But what if these principles don't seem to work with a particular child?

I reared four children and one of them had an especially difficult time with self-control, much more than his other three siblings. His actions were impulsive and spontaneous. He was not disobeying deliberately. On the contrary, he was a sweet-natured child with a heart as big as all outdoors. He just had a problem with impulse control and more often than not, he acted before he thought about the consequences of those actions. He wanted to be good; he just had a difficult time with it. Nevertheless, his actions needed to be corrected. Sometimes they were even dangerous. If there was a button, he pushed it; a knob, he turned it. Self-restraint did not come easy for him. Once he even opened the car door as we drove down a highway because I had not thought to tell the children not to open doors while the car was moving.

I wasn't sure what to do with this child. He spent much of his preschool years sitting in a time-out chair. I was a frustrated mom, feeling like I was constantly scolding this child and worried about my biblical responsibility to do just that.

Then, one day, I complained about my frustration to my friends at a church women's group. One of the ladies shared another biblical principle with me. This friend asked if I knew what Solomon, the wisest man who ever lived, said to his son. His comment can be found in Proverbs 23:26

where Solomon said, "My son, give me your heart" (NIV).

Seeking a child's heart is different from demanding obedience. We are asking our children to give us their hearts. If a person is forced to give something, then it is not a gift. Winning a child's heart requires wooing it. This puts the parents in a vulnerable position. Rather than issuing harsh demands as we sometimes do when requesting obedience, wooing a heart requires gentleness. This biblical principle provides a wonderful balance to the insistence on honor and obedience needed for good parenting.

In my parenting, it gave me a new perspective on disciplining this son. Yes, I still held him to standards, but I found myself doing it more gently, always trying to make sure he knew it was out of love. And I readily accepted his apologies. Instead of focusing so much on punishment for his infractions, I worked with him on ways to help him think before he acted.

He is grown now, and I can truly say his father and I won his heart. He has outgrown his childish impulsivity and grown into a successful man. Now he not only has a good relationship with us, he also loves the God we love and seeks to serve our God with his life.

Prayer: Heavenly Father, teach us to be gentle parents. Remind us daily of Your love and forgiveness toward us so that we may extend the same to the children You have blessed us with. In Your Son's name, Amen.

Thought for the Day: What children do you interact with on a regular basis? How can you woo their little hearts today?

Day 2: Where is Home?

by Shirley
Read: Philippians 2:12-18

O LORD, there is none like you to help,
between the mighty and the weak.
Help us, O LORD our God,
for we rely on you,
and in your name
we have come against this multitude.
O LORD, you are our God; let not man
prevail against you.
2 Chronicles 14:11

At a Christian Writer's Conference, I met someone who asked, "Where's home?" Before I was even aware I was speaking, I said, "Nigeria." I guess the confused look on his face alerted me to my answer. Then, I said, "Heaven." Another confused look. Then I said, "The States." Another confused look. Finally, I said, "Birmingham." No confused look. I explained that my parents were missionaries and I was born in Nigeria, West Africa. Then I saw a spark of understanding.

My family left Nigeria about fifty years ago, yet Nigeria is still home to me. As I think about it, I am not sure why I answered Nigeria. The country itself and the memories of precious Nigerians and missionaries and friends certainly are dear to me. But home was the place my parents made for our family. It wasn't a specific place on the map. Maybe that's a missionary-mindset thing. Wherever we were was home. I learned to create home where I was—in Nigeria it was Keffi, Lagos, Ogbomoso. In the States, it was Birmingham and Gadsden, Alabama, Nashville, Tennessee, and Annandale, Virginia.

There is a place where I keep my stuff, come back to at night, and leave from in the mornings as I head out to work—I call that home. Mom taught me to make people feel at home wherever I am. So, when I'm in my office and someone comes in, I want them to feel at home. When I meet someone at a restaurant for a meal, I want them to feel at home. When a visitor comes to church, I want them to feel at home.

Home, as defined by Merriam Webster, is "a place of residence," "a familiar setting," or "a place of origin." Home is a place where you are safe, loved, and comfortable.

In my mind, the structure in which you live is a house. I have known many people related to each other who lived together in a structure that was not really a home.

I have come to understand two important things about home:

1. Nowhere on earth is my eternal home—that place awaits me when I take my last breath here on earth.

2. Home is more of a sense of acceptance, understanding, unconditional love—as much as we are able to love each other unconditionally by the grace of God—encouragement, rest, relaxation, and even admonishment and correction. Home is a place where all of the family can thrive in their relationship with God and each other.

God has placed us on this earth for a reason, and that includes having a place to rest and restore spiritually, emotionally, mentally, and physically.

Yet, in the world in which we live, how can we really have rest when there is so much turmoil and chaos?

The hymn, "We Rest on Thee," written by Edith G. Cherry, answers the question of how we can have rest—we rest on God! The fourth verse speaks to this issue:

> We rest on Thee, our Shield and our
>   Defender!
> We go not forth alone against the foe;
> Strong in Thy strength, safe in Thy
>   keeping tender,
> We rest on Thee, and in Thy Name we go.

That is precisely how we can be at home and help others feel at home in this world in which we live—we rest on God!

The third verse of "We Rest on Thee" reminds us of our eternal home:

> We rest on Thee, our Shield and our
>   Defender!
> Thine is the battle, Thine shall be the

praise;
When passing through the gates of pearly
    splendor,
Victors, we rest with Thee, through
    endless days.

Romans 4:1 says, "Therefore, since the promise of entering his rest still stands, let us be careful that none of you be found to have fallen short of it."

Are you ready to pass "through the gates of pearly splendor?" What a glorious day when a Christ-follower goes home to heaven to eternally rest with God!

Prayer: Heavenly Father, thank You for the rest that You give us here on earth and the promise of eternal rest with You in heaven. Teach us to rest in You. In Jesus' name, Amen.

Thought for the Day: God's rest is for us here on earth and for eternity.

Day 3: God's Delight

by Harriet
Read: Zephaniah 3:17-20

The Lord is in your midst,
a mighty one who will save;
He will rejoice over you with gladness,
He will quiet you by His love; He will
exult over you by His love.
Zephaniah 3:17 (NIV)

So far in my life, I have only two grandchildren. Two of my sons are not married yet, so I may someday have more grandchildren, but right now, at the time I am writing this book, I have only two—a boy and a girl. The boy is the child of my daughter and the girl is the child of my second-oldest son.

My daughter and grandson lived in the same city as me for the first five years of his life, so I had the blessing of babysitting him often when he was an infant. Some days, I would watch him late into the night if my daughter had to work late. He is now eleven years old and they live in a city about an hour away from me because she found a job there, but even now, I keep him for weeks at a time during his school breaks.

My grandchildren delight me. This verse in Zephaniah shows me that God feels about His children the way I feel about my precious grandchildren. I rejoice over them with gladness; God rejoices over us with gladness. Sometimes after I had put my grandson to sleep when he was a baby, he would wake up crying from a bad dream. When I would hear him, I would tiptoe into the room where he slept, pick him up from his crib, carry him to the nearby rocking chair, and hold him close while I rocked him. I quieted him with my love as God quiets us with His love.

My grandchildren amuse me. When my granddaughter tries to drink from her sippy cup, she sometimes gets milk all over her. Instead of getting frustrated, she laughs and blows bubbles in her milk. She makes me laugh and I exult over her in my love for her. God exults over us in His love.

How precious it is to realize that God delights

in His family like I delight in mine. And actually, God's delight is far greater because He is capable of greater love than I am. My love for my family is merely a reflection of God's love for us.

Prayer: Heavenly Father, thank You for Your deep and abiding love for us. Thank You for exulting over us, rejoicing over us, and quieting us with Your love! How precious that Your family includes people of all colors and backgrounds! Teach us to share Your love with others. In Jesus' name, Amen.

Thought for the Day: The God of the Universe delights in us!

Day 4: To Whom Do You Belong?

by Shirley
Read: Ephesians 4:1-7

*I therefore ... urge you
to walk in a manner worthy of the calling
to which you have been called
with all humility and gentleness,
with patience,
bearing with one another in love ...*
Ephesians 4:1-3

My Great-Granddaddy Thomason's family reunion is every spring. When my mom, eighth of nine children, was growing up, her siblings and all the cousins were very close. Through the years they have tried to stay connected through the annual Thomason Family Reunion.

All of us are getting older and the children (my generation and following) do not seem quite as interested in staying connected with each other. Of course, much of our extended family is spread out across the country.

Mom always made sure I knew about the

reunions and when she got to where she couldn't drive, I made sure to take her. It was so interesting. When Mom reconnected with her cousins it was like the clock turned back to their childhood as they giggled and laughed about things they got into "back then," as they called it.

When I lived away from Birmingham and was not able to attend the reunions regularly, Mom would call and update me on what everyone was doing—as if I knew who the grandchildren of her third cousin, second-removed, even were.

As Mom's cousins get older and die, our reunion numbers dwindle. But we still get together. Without fail, someone will come up to me during the reunion and ask, "Who do you belong to?" They want to know exactly where on the family tree I fit and how we're connected to each other. One cousin has gone back and traced our ancestry forty-five generations.

To properly answer this question I have to say, I am the daughter of Jeannie Thomason Crowder, who is Olin Thomason's daughter. Now they know exactly to whom I belong.

Family is important. Mom used to say that

when she and her sisters were leaving the house to go somewhere, their mother would tell them, "Remember who you are." She meant, "When you go out into the world you are representing the Olin Thomason family. We have a certain standard of acceptable behavior by which we expect you to abide."

When I was growing up, my mom would say, "Remember whose you are." I was to represent the Ray Crowder family in accordance to the standards of acceptable behavior by which I was expected to abide. But she also intimated that I was a child of God. She gave me these instructions even before I came to faith in Christ, but she still expected me to act like a child of God, so people knew to whom I belonged.

I understood exactly what she meant. I wasn't to go to any wild parties or do any number of other things. Once I became a Christ-follower, I began to understand that it is not just what you say and how you act that matters. The important thing is that your heart's desire is to honor God.

How do Christ-followers ensure that our behavior does not reflect badly on God?

Jesus answered a Pharisee's question about which commandment was the greatest by saying, "You shall love the Lord your God with all your heart and with all your soul and with all your mind. This is the great and first commandment. And a second is like it: You shall love your neighbor as yourself. On these two commandments depend all the Law and the Prophets" (Matthew 22:37-40).

Then in John 13:34-35, Jesus said, "A new commandment I give to you, that you love one another: just as I have loved you, you also are to love one another. By this all people will know that you are my disciples, if you have love for one another."

Since you can't go wrong agreeing with Jesus, I'll say the way to ensure that our behavior does not reflect badly on God is to love God with our entire being and to love people. Well, that sounds easy … not! Why not? Because some people are more difficult to love than others, and none of us are easy to love all the time. But Jesus didn't say we are to love only the people who are easy to love—then who would love us at times? He said love everyone all the time.

We can only truly love people when we truly love God. Loving God means being obedient to His commands, spending time with Him in prayer, and through studying His Holy Spirit-inspired Bible.

My mom would say it like this, "When you love God first, it's easier to love people—even the difficult ones."

Do people know you belong to God by the way you love Him and them?

Prayer: Heavenly Father, it amazes us that we belong to You. What an incredible mercy and grace You have shown us. Help us know You better so that we will serve and represent You well to all the world. In Jesus' name, Amen.

Thought for the Day: Christ-followers belong to God and represent Him wherever we go and with whatever we do and say.

Day 5: Catch the Fire!

by Harriet
Read: Romans 10:13-15

*Therefore go
and make disciples of all nations,
baptizing them in the name of the Father
and of the Son and of the Holy Spirit.*
Matthew 28:19 (NIV)

It was a time of great spiritual awakening. If you lived during this time period, you would have felt the fire of evangelism sparking in the hearts of many around you. You might have been caught up in the fire yourself. I am referring to a series of evangelical awakenings that occurred from around the early 1800s through the 1960s. During this time, tens of thousands of men and women left the comforts of life—their homes and hearths—in Europe or America to travel to the remotest parts of the earth to take the light of salvation to those who lived in spiritual darkness.

Many of those brave individuals died at sea, or

in the jungles of Africa and South America, or at the hands of the very people they had abandoned everything to help. Still, they went. Their fire was contagious, their sacrifices not in vain, and thousands upon thousands heard the gospel and came to salvation because of them. Some of missions' great heroes come to my mind: Adoniram Judson of Burma, Hudson Taylor and Lottie Moon of China, David Livingstone of Africa, Jim Elliott and his brave coworkers in Ecuador ... just to name a few.

Shirley and I were children of this great evangelical movement. Our parents were among the courageous men and women who left everything, crossing a vast ocean to an unknown land because of their passion for the souls of people they had never met. We owe our wonderful childhood memories of growing up in Africa to this movement. But more than that, we owe our passion for missions to the brave men and women who belonged to the generations before us.

In Revelation 3:8 (NIV) God tells the church in Philadelphia, "I have placed before you an open door that no one can shut...." The generations before me had an open door too. Theirs was a great calling and many heeded it. It was a calling filled with adventure, challenge, love for their fellow man, and the joy of seeing God move and lost souls saved.

Today, our door to missions and evangelism is not as open any longer. In fact, new doors close to missions seemingly every day. I stood at the feet of the last generation that had an open door to foreign missions. I saw their zest for the Lord and the courage it required in the face of difficulties. The Nigeria mission where I grew up faced the Biafran War. My parents and missionary aunts and uncles witnessed the genocide of the Igbo people, the constant presence of armed soldiers, sudden evacuations, and the fear that the war could be in their front yard at any time. Yet they stayed their course, loving the hurting people around them and leading many to Christ.

This chapter is entitled "Home and Hearth." The fires we usually think of when we hear those words are the warm fires we set in the fireplaces of our homes during the cold winter months. These fires bring warmth, comfort, and remind us of family. But they always make me think of the fire in the hearts of men and women who traveled so far from the comforts of home for the sake of the gospel.

So, come away with me now. Imagine you are climbing aboard a boat bound for a foreign land that you have only known from books and lectures. You don't know how to speak the language, you have only a sketchy understanding of the culture, and no idea of what lies ahead. You have said goodbye to the family you love and will not see them again for several years. You look back and see the coastline fading from view behind you. You turn your gaze forward. A salty mist hits your face as the breeze blows through your hair. A grand adventure beckons you. There are places to go, people to meet, and souls in need of a Savior.

Prayer: Heavenly Father, we give You thanks for the brave men and women who sacrificed so much so that others could hear about Your love. Stir our hearts to want to reach others with the gospel, even today in our changing world, and show each one of us how You want us to work in Your kingdom. In

Jesus' name, Amen.

Thought for the Day: Has God set your heart on fire for Him? Then let that fire guide and inspire you today.

Chapter 7

God's World

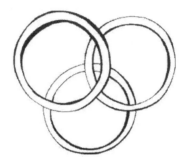

Day 1: The Earth is the Lord's

by Shirley
Read: Psalm 24

*The earth is the Lord's
and the fullness thereof,
the world and those who dwell therein.*
Psalm 24:1

Sitting in the food court at the student center of a college, I overheard a group of students talking about the earth. Each student in the group started a sentence with "Our world …" and followed that with a fact about the earth. I was interested in hearing the things they had to say about what they called "our world." They talked about global warming, pollution—air, land, and water—and various other environmental and ecological problems. Not one student mentioned anything positive or beautiful about their world. No one mentioned God. Perhaps this was a study or discussion group of some sort, but they totally missed the most important point about the earth.

It is indeed our world since we live on the

earth; however, it is God's world, for He made everything. The Bible begins with God creating His world, "In the beginning, God created the heavens and the earth" (Genesis 1:1). All that we see did not come into being by a big bang, it all came about through the design and creation of the Master Designer, God. "And God saw everything that he had made, and behold it was very good" (Genesis 1:31).

We see glimpses of God in creation and learn about Him by the things we observe. Romans 1:19-20 (NASB) says, "For since the creation of the world God's invisible qualities—his eternal power and divine nature—have been clearly seen, being understood from what has been made, so that people are without excuse." We glimpse God's invisible attributes in and through creation.

We glimpse God's glory in the sheer enormity of the universe. Mount Everest, the Challenger Deep in the Pacific Ocean, planets, countless stars, and the limitlessness of space show the splendor of God's glory.

We glimpse God's power in creation in earthquakes, tornadoes, hurricanes, and volcanoes.

These powerful things point us to the omnipotent God who created them.

We glimpse God's creativity in creation through graceful hummingbirds, colorful Bird of Paradise flowers, the complexity of the human body, and yes, even through vampire bats. All of these point to a creative God.

We glimpse God's beauty in sunrises and sunsets, rainbows, a mountain stream or a waterfall, the smile of a nonagenarian. In all of these, we can see a reflection of the beauty of their—and our—Creator God.

We glimpse God's goodness through many things: the sun that rises in the morning and sets in the evening, gravity, the air we breathe, and crops that provide food. All of these reflect the goodness of God.

We glimpse God's love in the way parents—human and animal—care for their children, the way the earth provides for the needs of all animals, the beauty we enjoy, and the way He sustains and controls the world. God's love is reflected in these and so many other ways.

Although my finite little mind cannot grasp the

full magnificence of God's world, I stand in awe of Creator God as creation reveals His attributes and I learn more about Him. God has entrusted human beings with caring for the world, even knowing that some would abuse it and claim it as their own. Nevertheless, He sustains it, as we read in Colossians 1:17, "He is before all things, and in Him all things hold together." And we have the privilege of living in God's magnificent world.

Prayer: Creator God, thank You for allowing us to live in Your beautiful world. Help us to take time to recognize Your glory, power, creativity, beauty, goodness, and love through Your creation so that we are reminded to sing praises to You. In the name of Jesus, Amen.

Thought for the Day: "If created things are seen and handled as gifts of God and as mirrors of His glory, they need not be occasions of idolatry—if our delight in them is always also a delight in their Maker." –John Piper

Day 2: My Father's World

by Harriet
Read: John 1:1-5

*Through him all things were made;
without him nothing was made that has
been made.*
John 1:3 (NIV)

This is my Father's world, and to my
    listening ears
All nature sings, and round me rings the
    music of the spheres.
This is my Father's world: I rest me in the
    thought
Of rocks and trees, of skies and seas;
His hand the wonders wrought.

Maltbie D. Babcock's hymn, "This is My
Father's World," takes me back to the Vacation
Bible Schools of my childhood, where I first
learned this song. At the time I was a child of
Africa, the place of my birth, where I lived for the

first ten years of my life and experienced my childhood. I loved Vacation Bible School back then and looked forward to it every year. It always happened during our mission's annual gathering that we called Mission Meeting. Mission Meeting itself was an exciting time for all the missionary kids since our families all gathered in one place. It was an opportunity to see friends we didn't get to see as often as we would have liked because our families were spread out all over Nigeria.

Vacation Bible School gave us children an activity to keep us occupied while our parents held their meetings. They took turns serving in Bible school, so they could also attend most of the planning meetings. Bible school always had opening and closing assemblies where we sang hymns. When I sang this song with its vivid lyrics about rocks and trees, and skies and seas, my mind's eye pictured a tropical world like the one familiar to me at that time in my life. My thoughts back then filled with canaries, parrots, lizards, chameleons, monkeys, tall palm trees, and rock formations as big as mountains—all of which I had seen in my young life.

Today, however, I have experienced other beautiful parts of God's world. Now I know of the breathtaking beauty of a crisp fall evening when the leaves are full of color and the moon hangs like a giant pumpkin in the sky, or a warm spring day when flowers burst open everywhere, both on the ground and in the trees. And I know the coziness of a sizzling fire in an open fireplace when the view through frosty windowpanes shows a heavy sky pouring snow so fast that the world is beginning to look like an iced cake before my eyes, or a winter's day after the storm clouds have cleared, when the bright sun glistens off a snowy white wonderland while the air nips at my ears and nose.

In Psalm 50:10-12 (NIV), God says, "every animal of the forest is mine, and the cattle on a thousand hills. I know every bird in the mountains, and the insects in the fields are mine … for the world is mine, and all that is in it."

The world is God's and all that is in it. What a comforting thought! Whether tropical, as I pictured it when I sang this song as a child in Nigeria, or frigid like the winters I have come to know today, whether jungle, forest, pastureland, or desert, it is all my Father's world!

Prayer: Heavenly Father, Creator of the Universe, we praise and honor You. Thank You for the beautiful world You have created. Teach us to appreciate the works of Your hands. In Your Son's name, Amen.

Thought for the Day: God's world is beautiful, and He has given it to us freely for our enjoyment.

Day 3: All Things Bright and Beautiful

by Shirley
Read: Genesis 1:1-4, 26-31

*And God saw everything
that he had made,
and behold, it was very good.*
Genesis 1:31

As a child, I learned Cecil Frances Alexander's hymn, "All Things Bright and Beautiful." I remember one teacher holding up pictures— remember, this was in the days before video—of each thing mentioned in the hymn. This hymn helped shape my understanding of Creator God.

Mrs. Alexander wrote "a number of hymn texts on articles of the Apostles' Creed" (hymnary.org) so she could help children understand their meaning. This hymn explains the phrase "Maker of heaven and earth" and is based on today's key passage: "And God saw everything that he had made, and behold, it was very good."

All of God's children—regardless of age—

understand from this hymn that "the Lord God made" everything as Genesis chapters one and two describe. Psalm 104:5 also tells us "He set the earth on its foundations, so that it should never be moved."

The verses of this beautiful hymn describe many delightful features of creation: flowers, birds, mountains, rivers, sunsets, light of morning, ripe fruits, trees, and meadows. With the mention of each feature, we learn God made the glowing colors of flowers, the tiny wings of birds, and everything else. "[God] made them all." Psalm 95:4-5 reiterates this fact: "In his hand are the depths of the earth; the heights of the mountains are his also. The sea is his, for he made it, and his hands formed the dry land."

One verse says:

The rich man in his castle,
The poor man at his fate,
God made them high and lowly,
And ordered their estate.

Here we are reminded that God is sovereign

and all of mankind is made by God, which gives each human life value. God not only created everything in the world, including mankind, He is intimately involved in and directs everything that happens in the world. "The mind of man plans his way, but the LORD directs his steps" (Proverbs 16:9 NASB).

The chorus reminds us:

All things bright and beautiful,
All creatures great and small,
All things wise and wonderful,
The Lord God made them all.

God made all creatures from the single-cell paramecium to the very complex human being. Everything that God created has value and a purpose even if we don't understand that value and purpose. God made everything that is wise and wonderful.

In the last verse we are told:

God gave us eyes to see them,
And lips that we might tell,

How great is God Almighty,
Who has made all things well.

Not only did God create all these bright and beautiful things, He gave us eyes so that we could see and experience them. God reveals His glory through creation (Isaiah 6:3). God loves, sustains, and directs creation as the Apostle Paul reminds us, "And he is before all things, and in him all things hold together" (Colossians 1:17).

Once we see God's creation as glimpses of who God is, our due response is thanksgiving and sharing about Him. In Ecclesiastes 3:14 (CSB) we read, "I know that everything God does will last forever; there is no adding to it or taking from it. God works so that people will be in awe of him." Psalm 136 is about all the things God created and the ways He protects and cares for His people. The psalm concludes with, "Give thanks to the God of heaven, for His steadfast love endures forever" (Psalm 136:26).

The words of another wonderful hymn, "For the Beauty of the Earth," by Folliott S. Pierpoint, seem to express an appropriate response of creation to Creator God:

> Lord of all, to Thee we raise,
> This our hymn of grateful praise.

Prayer: Creator God, thank You for the wonder of Your bright and beautiful creation. Thank You for the reminders of who You are and what You have done for us. Thank You for giving people the inspiration and talent to write beautiful hymns of faith that teach us deep biblical truths. In Jesus' name, Amen.

Thought for the Day: Listen and watch for creation to reveal aspects of God's character and join creation's choir as it sings praises to Creator God.

Day 4: The Eyes of the Lord

by Harriet
Read: 2 Chronicles 16:7-9

*For the eyes of the Lord move to and fro
throughout the earth
that He may strongly support those whose
heart is completely His.*
2 Chronicles 16:9a (NASB)

"It's like the radar in my airplane!"

With that exclamation and with excitement in his voice, my late father-in-law, David, showed a new Bible verse he had just discovered to his wife. He went on to explain, "You know the radar in my airplane? I see it in front of me on the plane's front panel every time I fly. It constantly sweeps back and forth searching for obstacles and storms that might be in my path as I fly, so I can fly safely. This verse I found says God's eyes are like that—like my radar! God's eyes, too, are constantly moving back and forth across the whole earth ... searching for things. But God's eyes are not looking for obstacles and storms, they are looking for hearts that love Him and are completely committed to Him. God searches these out so that He can strongly support them. Isn't that amazing? It sure makes me want to be a person with that kind of heart!"

David was a pilot who owned Michael-Walters Industries, a small business that made oil and grease for coal mining machinery. As Michael-Walters had plants in three states, he used his company's small twin-engine airplane to travel to the various plants. Every time he flew, he relied on the plane's radar. When he discovered this verse in Scripture, he could immediately relate to it, and it became one of his favorite verses. At one time he had the verse displayed in his office. His family still associates the verse with him, although he died many years ago.

David was a man whose heart belonged completely to God. How about you and me? Do we want to see God's strong support and faithful help in our lives? This is what 2 Chronicles 16:9 tell us will happen if ours is one of the hearts found by God's radar eyes.

It's the dead of winter. It's cold. There are

those in our midst dealing with difficult situations. Depression is often worse in the winter when we get less exposure to sunlight because of the shortened days. Many face higher utility bills and some have to choose between keeping their heat on or having food on their table. You might read this devotion and think that I have had an easy life since my father-in-law owned a business and an airplane. That is far from true. He passed away when my husband was only sixteen, and in the over thirty-nine years my husband and I have now been married, we have faced a business failure, family crises, and other hardships. But through it all, his father's favorite verse has brought us comfort.

The title of this chapter is "God's World." How comforting to know that no matter where in this cold, winter world we might be or whatever circumstances we might face, God's eyes can find us as He actively searches for men and women whose hearts love Him completely. How wonderful to have such a heart—one found by God's searching eyes!

Prayer: Thank You for Your promises. Thank You

for the strong support You show people whose hearts are completely Yours. Father, give us hearts for You. In the name of Christ, Amen.

Thought for the Day: I've heard it said that when God looks into our hearts, He wants to see His reflection. What can you do today to ensure that?

Day 5: God's Classroom

by Shirley
Read: Psalm 148:1-14

*For what can be known about God is
plain to them, because God has
shown it to them.
For his invisible attributes,
namely, his eternal power
and divine nature,
have been clearly perceived,
ever since the creation of the world,
in the things that have been made.
So they are without excuse.*
Romans 1:19-20

I found handwritten notes from a sermon on creation. I don't know when it was preached or who preached it, but they gave me a good start for this devotional. The notes begin with a question, "Did you know we are all in a classroom from the time we are born until we die? We are in God's classroom—the world." For someone who loves learning, this is an exciting idea! I am in a classroom where I am (or should be) learning all the time.

Several years ago, I was counseling a thirty-something, never-married, single woman with whom I had met twice before. She had skirted around the "I'm single but want to be married" issue in the previous sessions. During our conversation that day, I responded to something she said with, "Your theology of marriage needs some correcting. Let's see what the Bible has to say about it."

Her quick response was, "I hate theology, let's just look at the Bible."

While I realize that everyone is not a theology nerd like me, I am disturbed to find many Christ-followers of all ages who don't really understand what theology is. They think it is reserved for seminary students and preachers, not for ordinary Christ-followers.

So, before we go any further, let's define theology. Dr. Howard Eyrich defines theology as "the gathering of the teaching of the whole Bible on any given subject." My dad would explain it this way: "Theology about marriage (since I used the example above) is pulling together everything the

Bible says—from the Old and New Testaments—about marriage. That compilation is the theology of marriage."

We start with a definition of theology because if our theology is wrong, then our understanding of God and everything else is wrong. So, in God's classroom—the world—we study and learn theology—what the Bible teaches about the world. The Holy Spirit-inspired Bible and God's world are our instructors and required reading.

The prerequisites for this course are simple: anyone can be in this class, but you will have a significant advantage in learning and understanding the material if you know the instructor, God.

God's world testifies to the fact that there is indeed a God who created everything in an orderly fashion. Psalm 97:6 tells us, "The heavens proclaim his righteousness, and all the peoples see his glory."

Nature (the world) and God are not one and the same. God created nature. My understanding of the Bible is that God reveals Himself through creation; it shows us things about God. Nature provides information or facts about God's existence, but it cannot teach us the fullness of who God is, how sin entered the world, how sinful man can be reconciled to holy God, or how to live a life of obedience to God. All of that comes from God's revelation of Himself in the Bible.

Creation in its vast array and order testifies to God as Creator, as we read in Psalm 8:3: "When I look at the heavens, the work of your fingers, the moon and the stars, which you have set in place …"

Throughout the Bible, God tells us to learn about Him and our relationship to Him. He uses things in creation to teach us about Himself and how we are to live.

Let's look at the eagle to see some lessons God's classroom has for us from just one passage, Deuteronomy 32:10-12, that focuses on the gentleness and care the eagle gives to its eaglets. An eagle:

- protects and defends the eaglet.
- catches the eaglet when it falls.
- provides for the eaglet.
- watches over and never leaves the eaglet.

The eagle caring for its eaglet gives us a

glimpse of how God cares for and looks after His children (Christ-followers) in the same ways. God:

- protects and defends us (Deuteronomy 31:6, Psalm 5:11).
- catches us when we fall (Psalm 37:24, Psalm 145:14).
- provides for us (Matthew 6:25-34, Romans 8:32).
- watches over and never leaves us (Isaiah 41:10, Ephesians 3:16-17).

Isaiah 40:31 also tells us that "They who wait for the LORD shall renew their strength; they shall mount up with wings like eagles; they shall run and not be weary; they shall walk and not faint." From this, we learn that through a relationship with God and our hope and faith in Him, we receive a new ability to get with it and run the course of life.

Prayer: Creator God, we thank You for the lessons we learn in Your classroom—the world. Thank You for creating such a beautiful and interesting world for us to enjoy. As we stand in awe of Your creation, may it lead us to want to know You more and to be obedient to Your commands. In Jesus' name, Amen.

Thought for the Day: Look for glimpses of God as you interact with His creation. Then praise God for who He is.

Chapter 8

Love is in the Air

Day 1: God's Valentine

by Harriet
Read: Psalm 103:2-5

*I have loved you
with an everlasting love ...*
Jeremiah 31:3

So, Valentine's Day is coming around again. It's that special day in the year when we celebrate love. In particular, we celebrate a certain kind of love—the love between two people—a man and a woman. Sadly, though, there are some who do not have a love interest in their lives on this day.

My niece is married and a teacher now, but she has an undergraduate degree in drama, and she can be quite funny. A few years ago, when she was still in college and single, I happened to be with her on Valentine's Day as she complained of being alone on that day. She went into a funny impromptu monologue comparing Valentine's Day to a really bad audition.

Stepping onto an imaginary stage, and then pretending to address an audience, my niece began to explain it this way, "When you go to an audition, you walk into a room full of people who also want the part you are hoping to get. But in a normal audition, you know that everyone in this crowded room is going to go home empty-handed except for one person. Only one will be cast in the role that everyone in the room is hoping for, and everyone else will be disappointed. Valentine's Day, on the other hand, is like a really bad audition, because here, everyone in the crowded room is hoping for a card, or candy, or flowers, but in this audition, four out of every five will win! And there you are ... among the minority who doesn't get that card, candy, or flowers. You watch as the names of nearly everyone around you are called. But no, in the end, you find that you are part of the small group that goes home empty-handed."

This may sound sad, but it was hilarious at the time. My niece was melodramatic in her own impromptu comic routine speaking to her imaginary audience, and her real audience of two—her mother and I—loved it!

Yet, despite the humor, I think of her words every Valentine's Day. There is a poignant truth in them. This year I want to remind all those whose names will not be called in this really bad audition we call Valentine's Day. If you are a Christ-follower, you do have a love. His name is Jesus, and He is the lover of your soul. What He gives you and me is much better than cards, candy, or flowers. He gives us His everything. He purchased us for Himself with His blood.

The Bible tells us this in so many words when it says in John 3:16, "For God so loved the world, that He gave his only Son, that whoever believes in Him should not perish but have eternal life." Jesus loved you and me enough to die for us and He gives us the best gifts. Who needs cards, flowers, or candy? The lover of our souls gives us the gift of everlasting life!

Isaiah 38:17 (KJV) says, "but Thou hast in love to my soul delivered it from the pit of corruption: for Thou hast cast all my sins behind Thy back."

So, happy Valentine's Day! Don't forget the One who loves you most!

Prayer: Loving Father, on this day when we think of love, help us to remember that You love us with an everlasting love.

Thought for the Day: Meditate on the fact that God loves you more than any human is capable of.

Day 2: God's Love Heals, Protects, Overcomes

by Shirley
Read: 1 Corinthians 13

[Love] always protects, always trusts,
always hopes, always perseveres.
1 Corinthians 13:7 (NIV)

In my Bible, I wrote an outline of 1 Corinthians 13 from a sermon my dad preached many years ago. It is a simple five-word outline: God's love heals ... protects ... overcomes.

God loves His people with a love that is all-powerful, all-knowing, and ever-present. That love does not always spare us from tragedies or illnesses. When our circumstances appear hopeless, God is faithful. His love gives us the strength needed to walk through anything.

The world, and sadly many Christ-followers, do not understand biblical love. God is love (1 John 4:8) and God is the source of love (1 John 4:7). God extends His love to us (Ephesians 2:4). God's love is everlasting (Jeremiah 31:3). God's love is unconditional (Titus 3:4-5).

God's love heals. One of the names for God is Jehovah-Rapha—the God who heals. In Exodus 15:26b God says, "I am the LORD, your healer."

Sometimes, the healing of love may not look like you expect it to, but it is precisely the healing you need for God's glory and for your spiritual good. God's love heals us spiritually, emotionally, mentally, and physically.

God's powerful healing comes first to us as we put our faith and trust in Him as Savior and Lord (Hebrews 11:6). His healing comes when we have faith—even a tiny bit—that He is able to heal. Remember the woman in Matthew 9 who had hemorrhaged for twelve years? Jesus healed her because she put her faith in Him.

God calls Christ-followers to love others. As we love others, relationships are healed; we are compelled and propelled to serve others and sometimes help them heal from physical maladies.

God's love protects. God protects in ways that are not always how we want or expect to be protected, for at times we are not spared from disasters here on earth, but He gives us eternal life. The Lord directs everything for His glory and our ultimate spiritual good as He ensures Christ-followers' everlasting life in His presence. Romans 8:38-39 tells us that God's love protects us against separation from Himself. The story of Jonah shows God's protecting love that kept him from drowning in the sea and brought him safely back to land.

God calls Christ-followers to love others. As we love others, we are always watching and looking out for the good of those around us. We do all we can to protect them from things that can do them harm—spiritually, emotionally, mentally, and physically.

God's love overcomes. God's powerful love overcomes sin (Romans 8:1-4) and Jesus overcame the world (John 16:33). God's love overcomes fear (1 John 4:18). Because of God's love, we can overcome anything that may come against us (Romans 8:28). We are reminded in Romans 8:31, "If God is for us, who can be against us?" In the verses that follow in Romans 8:32-39, we understand that God is all-powerful and that no one or thing—the devil, law, tribulation, height, depth, or any other person or circumstance that comes to mind—can separate us from God's overcoming love. God's love is all-powerful, all-conquering, and everlasting.

God calls Christ-followers to love others. As we love others, we come alongside them to encourage and help them overcome and conquer the things with which they are struggling.

God's love heals … protects … overcomes. Anything other than that is not love!

Prayer: Loving Heavenly Father, teach us to love as You have loved us. Help us learn to walk in the freedom, strength, and grace of Your love. Make us aware of opportunities we encounter to show Your love to others. In Jesus' name, Amen.

Thought for the Day: We can walk in and through any situation with the confidence that God is with us, healing and protecting us, so that through Him we can overcome anything.

Day 3: The Greatest Love

by Harriet
Read: John 3:16-19

*Greater love has no one than this: to lay
down one's life for one's friend.*
John 15:13 (NIV)

A little eleven-year-old boy trudged along dirt roads as he walked the five miles from his school to the hospital in rural Africa. His sister was in the hospital and needed him to donate his blood to her. So, he walked … all five long miles of the trip.

Once at the hospital, he was told to lie down on a cot and the hospital personnel inserted an intravenous line into his little arm through which they withdrew his blood. After donating the blood, the little boy lay still on his cot. He did not get up. He just lay there … for a very long time. At first, the nurse thought perhaps he needed some extra rest; donating blood can sometimes weaken a person, after all, and he was just a child. But after a while, his stillness caught the eye of the missionary doctor. The doctor walked over to the little boy's cot and told him he could get up and walk back to school now if he felt like it.

But the little boy had a burning question on his mind. He looked up at the doctor and bravely asked, "When will I die?"

Of course, the doctor was surprised at the question and assured the little boy that donating blood would not cause him to die. A surprised but elated little boy sprang up from his bed, skipped out the door, and started his walk back to school.

I heard this true story from a missionary friend who worked at the little boy's school, a missionary friend I grew up calling uncle since the missionary kids called all the adult missionaries uncle or aunt. He had heard it from the missionary doctor who treated the boy and his sister. The sister got well, by the way, and was released from the hospital after some days.

The story pierced me deeply. The whole walk to the hospital, all five miles of it, the little boy thought he was giving his life to save his sister's life. I can picture it in my mind—this little boy walking a dirt path under the hot tropical sun, thinking it was his last walk on earth. And then when he had the IV placed in his arm and watched the blood leaving his body, he expected at any minute that he would be drawing his last breath. Yet he did not turn back. He kindly offered his blood for his sister, though he thought it would cost him his life. How great must have been his love for his sister! I have to wonder; do I have that kind of love for others? Jesus certainly did.

February, the month of love, comes in the middle of the stark, cold winter. Usually, we think of romantic love during this month, but love is love, whether romantic or brotherly. And to show love of any kind requires valuing someone else above ourselves. How is God asking you and me to show His love to others in this time of year when we think so much about love? Who is He calling us to love? What specific things can we do to share God's love with someone?

Prayer: Heavenly Father, I do not know if I am capable of having that kind of sacrificial love for others, but I do know that Jesus had that kind of love for me. Teach me to love sacrificially and to share Your love with others. In Jesus' name, Amen.

Thought for the Day: Jesus demonstrated the greatest love when He laid down His life for us.

Day 4: As I Have Loved You

by Shirley
Read: John 13:31-38

A new commandment I give to you,
that you love one another:
just as I have loved you,
you also are to love one another.
By this all people will know
that you are my disciples,
if you have love for one another.
John 13:34-35

I was around nine years old when our Training Union memory verse was John 13:34. I worked hard all week to learn it word for word. I wrote it out on paper and practiced it over and over until I could say it without messing up or needing help with any of the words. I was so proud of myself that evening as I stood and quoted the passage in front of the others in my Training Union class. I received another sticker on my Bible memory verse card and couldn't wait to brag about it to my mom and dad.

Once everyone was in the car heading home

after church, I made sure that Mom, Dad, and my brother Tim knew I had earned another sticker.

When we got home, I was supposed to help Mom get supper ready. I didn't think someone who had earned a Bible memory verse sticker should have to set the table, but I obeyed—not very joyfully, though.

After supper, Mom and I were washing dishes. She asked me to quote my memory verse for her. I did. Then she asked me to explain what it meant. "Huh?" I thought, "I had to memorize it, not know what it means!"

I learned a good deal about what biblical love is and isn't that night. I also learned that just memorizing a verse about love doesn't mean anything if I don't love God and others.

Today's passage takes place during what we call the Last Supper. After Jesus reveals that Judas would betray Him, Judas leaves Jesus and the other disciples.

Jesus speaks tenderly to the disciples, calling them "little children" and tells them they cannot go with Him (meaning to the cross). Jesus then introduces "a new commandment." He tells the disciples to "love one another just as I have loved you."

The disciples would have known the Old Testament command in Leviticus 19:18, "you shall love your neighbor as yourself." So why is this commandment new? The Old Testament Jews had forgotten that this command was dealing with the heart of man and not outward observance only.

The motivation for this new commandment was that we are to love others "as [God] loved you." How did God love us? "In this is love, not that we have loved God but that he loved us and sent his Son to be the propitiation for our sins. Beloved, if God so loved us, we also ought to love one another" (1 John 4:10-11).

This new commandment to love one another was tied to the command to love God. In fact, Jesus said that "the whole Law and the Prophets" depend upon these two commands (Matthew 22:34-40). It is also "new" because Jesus broadens the definition of "neighbor" as basically anyone with whom we cross paths—including our enemies.

When we are saved, "God's love [is] poured into our hearts through the Holy Spirit who has been given to us" (Romans 5:5). Love is also a fruit of the Spirit (Galatians 5:22) given to Christ-followers.

Biblical love is putting the needs, rights, and feelings of others before our own. It is speaking words that encourage others (1 Thessalonians 5:11).

Biblical love is a foundational characteristic of all true Christ-followers. I specify biblical here, because the culture has its own definition of love, which usually means being nice to someone. Biblical love includes "speaking the truth in love" (Ephesians 4:15), which includes confronting sin in another Christ-follower's life. Remember the biblical account of Nathan confronting King David with his sin (2 Samuel 12:1-7)?

Jesus continues by telling the disciples that instead of people knowing these men are His disciples because they follow Him around, they will now know them because they "love one another." One of many passages speaking of this is 1 John 4:7: "Beloved, let us love one another, for love is from God, and whoever loves has been born of God and knows God."

Prayer: Loving Heavenly Father, thank You for loving us and teaching us to love You and others. Help us better understand Your everlasting love for us, for it is only by understanding You and Your love that we can begin to know how to love You and others well. In Your Son's name, Amen.

Thought for the Day: Loving others is the outward manifestation of the love of God in the life of a Christ-follower. Does the way you love others indicate you are a Christ-follower?

Day 5: God's Love

by Harriet
Read: 1 John 4:7-12

Whoever does not love does not know
God, because God is love.
1 John 4:8 (NIV)

Men cleaning an insane asylum some three hundred years ago found words scrawled across the walls of a room that a recently deceased patient had once inhabited. One of the men was so moved by the words, he jotted them down and the inscription became a Jewish poem. The words read:

O love of God, how rich and pure!
How measureless and strong!
It shall forevermore endure
The saints' and angels' song.

Richard M. Lehman was a businessman living in California in the early 1900s. He worked in a packing house all day packing oranges and lemons into wooden crates for shipment to various places. But he was also a musician who loved the Lord. One day after reflecting upon a sermon he'd heard the previous Sunday, he was moved to write a song about God's love. He remembered the words to the old Jewish poem someone had written down for him and the story behind it. He looked around for the card where his friend had jotted it down.

Finding the card, he sat down at his piano and wrote two more stanzas to the song we now know as "The Love of God." Richard's daughter, Claudia L. Mays, arranged the tune. It was first published in 1919 in a songbook entitled, *Songs that are Different*:

Could we with ink the ocean fill
And were the skies of parchment made,
Were every stalk on earth a quill
And every man a scribe by trade,

To write the love of God above
Would drain the ocean dry,
Nor could the scroll contain the whole

Tho' stretched from sky to sky.

O love of God, how rich and pure!
How measureless and strong!
It shall forevermore endure
The saints' and angels' song.

The name of the man in the insane asylum is not known, but his words have been immortalized as the third stanza of this now-famous hymn. Both the story of the man in the insane asylum and the words of the song touch me deeply.

I have known and loved some people who have struggled with mental health issues. Conditions like bipolar and schizoaffective disorders, schizophrenia, severe anxiety, and other such health issues were not understood well or treated effectively 300 years ago. I am so thankful that today they are, and these dear loved ones of mine can lead functioning lives instead of being locked away in insane asylums.

The people I know who struggle with these mental health issues love God and are keenly aware of His great love for them. Sometimes struggling with these issues, or any chronic issue for that matter, can help sharpen our awareness of the fact that God loves us for who we are, not for the things the world values like health, intelligence, physical appearance, or earthly possessions. He loves the person who has received His gift of salvation regardless of their status in this world. And He loves them dearly! So dearly that if it were written down, scrolls could not contain the words, "tho' stretched from sky to sky."

Prayer: Gracious Heavenly Father, Your love is more precious than earthly treasures. It warms us, heals us, comforts us, and most importantly, saves us. Thank You for loving us. Draw us close to You today. In Jesus' name, Amen.

Thought for the Day: The unnamed man in the insane asylum wrote a powerful truth when he said that God's rich, pure love will endure forever. How marvelous!

Chapter 9

Live Peacefully

Day 1: Moment by Moment

by Shirley
Read: Philippians 4:1-9

You keep him in perfect peace whose mind
is stayed on you,
because he trusts in you.
Trust in the LORD forever, for the LORD
GOD is an everlasting rock.
Isaiah 26:3-4

As a child in Nigeria, I heard about and witnessed some of the things happening during one particular coup d'état. We missionary kids witnessed some horrible, gruesome things, as did our parents. I still can vividly conjure those bloody scenes in my mind's eye. There was much unrest and uncertainty. On the hospital compound where we lived in Ogbomoso, everyone prepared and was ready to make a quick escape from the compound if needed.

I remember suitcases placed at the front and back doors so that we would be able to grab a bag and run, regardless of which door we exited. I won't go into all the other details here, but I think I've said enough to give you an idea of the situation we were in. My sister Anne and brother Paul were at a boarding school in a different city, while my brother Tim and I were with Mom and Dad.

I was young then, so I didn't really understand the severity of all that was happening at the time, although I knew it was bad, because of the things I saw.

Yet, in all of those memories, I do not recall being afraid. In fact, I felt very safe. Now some of you may be thinking, "Sure you felt safe. You didn't know how much danger you were in." You're right, I didn't really understand. My brother Tim, who was a little older than me, was given instructions on what to do to help take care of Mom and me if we had to evacuate without Dad.

I'm sure my young age and lack of understanding were partly responsible for my lack of fear, but there was another reason.

While my mom was giving orders to everyone and making sure the right things were packed and so on, she was not in a panic. She was just being

Mom getting everyone ready for a trip and making sure everyone knew what they were supposed to be doing at the time and what they were to do when the trip began.

How did my mom and other missionaries have the presence of mind to know what needed to be packed and how to divide things so the bags at both doors held everything we would need? How did they go about making all of these preparations while showing the children and others around them they were not afraid?

The answer lies in another memory. Can you guess what memory is the clearest all these many decades later? No, it's not the man being brutally beaten and killed, it is my mom singing a hymn, and not one of the regular ones she hummed and sang all the time. Over and over she sang "Moment by Moment," by Daniel Whittle. Only certain phrases stuck in my mind:

- "Moment by moment, O Lord, I am Thine."
- "Moment by moment, I'm under His care."
- "Moment by moment He thinks of His

own."

- "Moment by moment, in woe or in weal, Jesus my Savior abides with me still."

How were my mom and the other missionaries able to do what they did? They had unwavering faith in God to help them. They knew that God was with them and would give them wisdom and discernment as to how they should prepare and care for their families. That faith gave them peace. I don't mean that the fighting or killing ended. I mean they were at peace with their Savior and Lord who had called them to Nigeria to tell about Him regardless of what was going on in their surroundings.

Because the peace of Christ ruled in my mom's heart (Colossians 3:15), she had peace. Because Mom had peace, I was not afraid. Now, I know that my experience is not the same as some of the other missionary kids, but by God's grace, I came to know the God of Peace as my Savior and Lord. I learned to trust Him and obey His commands so that during the uprisings of life, I can experience His peace moment by moment.

Prayer: Almighty God, thank You that through Your Son Jesus we can have salvation by which we have peace with You and can experience Your peace. Help us know You better so that we will trust in You and experience Your peace when our lives are in turmoil and we are afraid. In Jesus' name, Amen.

Thought for the Day: "And the peace of God, which surpasses all understanding, will guard your hearts and your minds in Christ Jesus" (Philippians 4:7).

Day 2: Peace

by Harriet
Read: John 14:23-27

Peace I leave with you;
my peace I give you.
John 14:27a (NIV)

I can remember it like it was yesterday. I stood with the other members of my senior class in high school, our backs against the walls on both sides of the auditorium as we made a large circle around the underclassmen and sang these words to those we were leaving behind when we graduated. We sang a version of these words, anyway.

My high school practiced an annual rite of passage. Every spring, just before graduation, the school had one last assembly in the auditorium, during which the seniors were both celebrated and teased in a verbal roasting. Each class in the high school had assigned seats in the auditorium, with the seniors closest to the stage, working back to the balcony where the youngest class sat. Every year, at the end of this last assembly, each class moved up to their new seats, except the seniors who vacated the coveted front seats they had so eagerly occupied the year before. They formed a large circle around the auditorium and then began singing this song of peace, based on John 14:27, "Peace I leave with you …" It was a poignant moment I will remember until my old age.

What a nice thought … to leave peace with your friends! If only we really had that power. What does peace mean? What does it mean in the eyes of the world and how is that different from the peace Jesus said he was leaving with His disciples?

When I think of peace through the world's eyes, images of the colorful 1960s come to my mind. I picture a long-haired man in bell-bottoms with a headband around his head, holding his hand up with his fingers in a V as he flashes the peace symbol. Somehow, I don't think this is what Jesus meant when he spoke of leaving His peace with His disciples.

God's peace is entirely different from the

world's peace. Though one may find many different definitions, at its core, peace is the concept of harmony and the absence of hostility. In the world's eyes, peace means the lack of hostility among people. In the 1960s they may have been motivated to speak of peace because of the hostilities of the Vietnam war, but at least in part, they were also urging for authority figures to allow them to freely do whatever they wanted, even things that were illegal, such as drugs. This is not God's peace.

God's peace can be experienced even in the midst of worldly, physical hostility. God's peace comes from an absence of God's anger and hostility toward our sins because of His forgiveness when we accept Christ as our Savior. God's peace comes from living in harmony with His will for our lives. This is the peace Jesus left with His disciples and us. As Christ-followers we can have this peace even in difficult circumstances. This is the peace that is sometimes referred to as the peace that passes understanding.

One of my son's best friends, whom he had known for many years at his Christian school, died suddenly as he was struck by a car when crossing the road. He was only sixteen. Though his friends and parents were grief-stricken beyond words, we had a sense of peace that the world would not understand. We knew he was a Christ-follower, so we knew he was in heaven, living eternally in perfect peace with a God who loves him. That is the peace Jesus left to His followers.

Prayer: Thank You, Father, for making peace with us through Jesus' death and resurrection. Help us to learn to be at peace in all our circumstances. In Jesus' name, Amen.

Thought for the Day: Christ died to make peace between us and the Father. As His followers, His peace is one of His sweet gifts to us.

Day 3: Peace, Be Still

by Shirley
Read: Mark 4:35-41

And he awoke and rebuked the wind
and said to the sea,
"Peace! Be still!"
And the wind ceased,
and there was a great calm.
Mark 4:39

I have never been on a boat during a storm, but I have been in an airplane way up in the sky when a storm hit. The turbulence shook and rocked the plane. I was certain that we were going to end up crashing in the ocean, even though we were over Nebraska!

I have also been driving my car in heavy traffic when a strong storm hit. The rain was falling sideways and the wind blowing so hard I had to fight to keep the car in the lane.

These are two of the terrifying things from my life that seem comparable to the incident in today's passage. The disciples and I registered very high on the terrified scale.

Let's look at the situation more closely. The disciples and Jesus got in a boat to go to the other side of the lake away from the crowds, even though the Bible says that other boats were with them. The lake was fairly deep, and because of the topography of the area sudden violent storms often occurred. Jesus was sleeping when the storm burst onto the scene and waves began breaking into their boat and filling it with water. Now remember, many of the disciples were fishermen who were used to storms, so this must have been a real doozy of a storm for it to have frightened them.

Matthew, Mark, and Luke recorded this incident, and as with most things reported by multiple witnesses, the dialogue varies a bit in each account. Regardless, they were basically saying, "Jesus, save us from drowning!"

Jesus woke up and reprimanded the wind and the sea by saying, "Peace! Be still!" The wind and sea obeyed and instantly were calm. Jesus then spoke to the disciples and asked why they were afraid, and He asked them where their faith was.

The disciples were "filled with great fear" and asked each other, "Who is this guy that the wind and sea obey Him?"

Here we see Jesus is fully man as His body requires rest and time away from the crowds. We also see Jesus is fully God when the wind and seas obey His command.

We see the disciples' faith wavering even though they were with Jesus when He healed people from diseases. They knew Him well. He reprimanded them for their lack of faith. In the same way, the Holy Spirit convicts us of our wavering faith when we face the storms of life.

We know Jesus calmed the wind and the seas, but don't miss the point that He also calmed the fears of the disciples. If Jesus can command the wind and seas to be peaceful and calm as well as calm the fears of the disciples, He most certainly is able to calm the storms that come into our lives. Every moment of every day we must choose whether to rest in God's promises or to worry ourselves sick trying to handle and fight against the storms we are facing.

I define peace as: the manifestation of the

presence and power of God in my life. Sometimes, I doubt God because I just cannot wrap my mind around who He is, what He does, and how He cares for me. Then I have to confess my sin, repent, and receive His forgiveness as I learn to trust Him more.

In what situations of your life is God saying, "Peace; be still"?

Prayer: Heavenly Father, forgive us for focusing on the turbulence and turmoil around us during the storms, instead of on You. Teach us to meditate upon Your word so that we are strengthened to trust You during the storms. Thank You for Your peace that calms our fears. In Jesus' name, Amen.

Thought for the Day: You can rest and have peace by trusting that God will fulfill His promises.

Day 4: Owudi

by Harriet
Read: Romans 10:9-13

*For there is no difference
between Jew and Gentile
—the same Lord is Lord of all and
richly blesses all who call on him ...*
Romans 10: 12 (NIV)

In February, we celebrate the life of Martin Luther King, a hero of the civil rights movement. Because of this, race relations is a hot topic during this month. I was a child during the time of Dr. King, but I did not live in America. My experience with prejudice centered around hostility between tribes rather than races.

Owudi came to live with us when I was a baby, to take care of me while my parents worked. I loved Owudi! Though she didn't speak my language well, she communicated her love in other ways, like playing with me, laughing, rocking me to sleep at night, and kissing my tears away when I cried.

Before becoming a Christian, Owudi was married and the mother of three young children. But when she chose a religion different from her husband's, he issued an ultimatum. She had to renounce her faith, or he would divorce her. In those days, a Nigerian woman gave up everything if she divorced. There were no divorce courts or lawyers to help her. She lost everything—her home, her husband, and her children—and was never allowed to see them again. She was banished!

So she came to work for us. While both of my parents worked at the hospital, my father as a physician and my mother as a nurse, Owudi stayed at our home with my siblings and me. She felt like a second mother to us. For her part, she was happy to be around children again. It made the loss of her children a little easier to bear. She poured her love on us.

After a few years, the mission moved my family, first to Oyo for language school and after that to Ogbomoso. Most of my childhood was spent in Ogbomoso, which is located in a different part of Nigeria. It's an area inhabited by a tribe that was different from Owudi's tribe, but she moved with us anyway and felt like a member of my family.

When I was ten, the Biafran war broke out, a difficult time for everyone in Nigeria. The Eastern part of Nigeria, where Owudi was from, waged war against the rest of the country in a futile attempt to gain independence. At its core, it was a tribal war. The Igbo tribe living in the East was at odds with the other tribes. The conflict hit home at our house because Owudi was Inguini, a small tribe closely related to the Igbos and supportive of their cause. But Ogbomoso, where we lived, was Yoruba land.

Fearing for Owudi's life, my parents arranged for her to travel back to her homeland. This was a wise and gracious move on the part of my parents, and God blessed it. Owudi made a safe journey back and lived many more years among her own people. But it was devastating to me!

I did not understand. My parents tried to explain that Owudi was in danger if she remained among the Yorubas. They tried their best to help me understand the term *prejudice*. I had never heard of it before, and I simply could not wrap my brain around the idea that one person might harm another just because of the tribe they belonged to (or the color of their skin, or all the other equally absurd reasons people have for hating each other). Owudi was the embodiment of love to me and I could not imagine why anyone would want to hurt her!

Jesus taught that there was no difference in people groups. That's what He meant when he said there was no difference between the Jew and the Greek. My father is a surgeon. I've heard him say that when you open someone up and see their insides, people are all the same. All people are made in the image of God, all sin, and all need a Savior.

Prayer: Oh Lord, You made us in Your image—all of us, male, female, and all colors and sizes. Help us learn to see people through Your eyes. In Jesus' name, Amen.

Thought for the Day: "If it is possible, as far as it depends on you, live at peace with everyone" (Romans 12:18 NIV).

Day 5: Is It Well With Your Soul?

by Shirley
Read: Philippians 4:5-9

*What you have learned and received
and heard and seen in me—
practice these things,
and the God of peace will be with you.*
Philippians 4:9

I can still remember the first time I laid eyes on my sweet friend Mrs. Mildred, whom I called Mrs. M. I was seated at the piano playing the prelude before the Sunday morning service began. It was a crisp winter morning and the sun shone brightly through the beautifully colored stained-glass windows. I turned the page in the hymnal and landed on the wonderful hymn, "There Is Sunshine in My Soul Today" by Eliza Hewitt, one of my mom's many favorite hymns.

I glanced toward the back of the worship center and saw the outward manifestation of the Son shining in the soul of a beautiful lady slowly making her way in. What I noticed about her was her radiant smile. It was only a few seconds later that I realized she was using a walker and seemed to be struggling as she walked.

After the service ended, I went to meet this lady, and there began my friendship with a precious octogenarian Christ-following lady. As I began to learn about her life and all the hardships she had endured and the stroke that had occurred some six months earlier, I said, "Oh, I am so sorry for all that you have been through. I know it has been difficult." Without hesitation, she grabbed hold of my hand and said, "Praise God! It is well with my soul!"

Space won't allow me to fill in the details of her interesting and difficult life. She would say, "I thank God He saved me when I was 60 years old. Imagine what a mess I would be by now if He had not!"

In the ten years that followed, I was blessed to walk alongside Mrs. M as her health declined and her only living relative, a grandniece, died. At age ninety-nine, she had another massive stroke. She was unable to communicate well during those last few days of her life here on earth but would mouth a few garbled words now and then.

When the doctor told me that it wouldn't be too long before Mrs. M died, I sat by her bedside with her Bible open and read from the Psalms. I told her that she would soon see her Savior. She struggled to whisper, "It is well. I … am … well."

How could this dear woman of God say "it is well" when so many things in her life had been devastating, even to the point of leaving her to live on the streets? Mrs. M would tell me, "Only by the grace of God!"

Once she became a Christ-follower, Mrs. M learned to study the Bible. She spent a great deal of time each day reading, studying, memorizing, meditating and contemplating upon the truths in the Bible, and praying. Her prayer list was comprehensive and handwritten on many pages. On the table by her rocking chair, you would find her prayer list sticking out of her well-worn Bible. The pages of her Bible—from Genesis 1:1 to Revelation 22:23—were covered with her handwritten notes.

One of Mrs. M's favorite Scripture passages was today's passage. She understood that when she was obedient to God's commands and she continually thought on the things that are worthy of praise (Philippians 4:8), it was indeed well with her soul.

I would often hear Mrs. M singing or humming Horatio Gates Spafford's hymn, "It Is Well with My Soul." She always sang all the verses followed by the chorus. The second verse was her favorite and she would belt it out loudly and triumphantly:

> Though Satan should buffet, though trials
>   should come,
> Let this blest assurance control:
> That Christ has regarded my helpless
>   estate,
> And has shed his own blood for my soul.

She would begin each chorus singing loudly and get softer with each line so that by the last line it was as if she were whispering a prayer: "It is well with my soul, It is well, it is well with my soul."

After singing the last phrase of the last chorus, with barely a break she would belt out the chorus of "Since Jesus Came into My Heart" by Rufus H.

McDaniel, as if it were an ending chorus to "It Is Well with My Soul."

> Since Jesus came into my heart,
> Since Jesus came into my heart,
> Flood of joy o'er my soul like the sea
> billows roll,
> Since Jesus came into my heart.

That's the answer, isn't it? Mrs. M had a personal relationship with her Savior and Lord Jesus, whom she trusted and in whom she had unwavering faith. Through His presence in her life she experienced the peace of God that allowed her to say, "It is well, it is well with my soul."

Prayer: Gracious Heavenly Father, thank You for Your presence which brings peace into our lives even when everything around us is in chaos. Help us learn to trust You more. In Jesus' name, Amen.

Thought for the Day: Are the things upon which you continually think building your faith and trust in God?

Chapter 10

Winter Things

Day 1: High Regard

by Harriet
Read: 1 Thessalonians 5:12-16

He has shown you, O mortal,
what is good.
And what does the LORD require of you?
To act justly and to love mercy
and to walk humbly with your God.
Micah 6:8 (NIV)

"Isn't he amazing? Did you see that shot? Wow! He sure can dunk the ball!"

It's the middle of basketball season for high schools and colleges in America. We're all cheering on our favorite team and making out our brackets, trying to guess which team we think will win the college national championship. But it's not only Americans who hold accomplished athletes in high regard. I grew up in Nigeria in the 1960s and can still remember hearing about Dick Tiger, a Nigerian boxer and the pride of Nigeria. I heard his name uttered from many lips—in the town market, in the villages, and from the men who worked at places I frequented, like the mission hospital and seminary.

"Dick Tiger could beat Cassius Clay!" the Nigerians proudly boasted. Though he never got in the ring with Cassius Clay, the man who later became known as Muhammad Ali and who is now considered to be one of the best boxers of all time, Tiger did hold championships in three countries in his career—Nigeria, England, and the US. And he made his countrymen proud with each one!

Watching a person defeat or help his or her team to defeat a rival on the court, field, or in the ring is certainly exciting. It gives us an adrenalin rush. We can't help but think highly of the athlete, especially if they play for the team we support. But is this who God tells us to hold in high regard?

The Bible gives other criteria for the traits or behavior that we should value. Today's passage in 1 Thessalonians says to value those who work hard, even those who admonish you in the Lord, because they are shaping you in the Lord. In Philippians 2:25-30, Paul tells of a man named Epaphroditus who had worked with him and cared for him. Paul calls this man a brother, co-worker, and fellow soldier and tells the people to hold him in high regard. And today's key verse says beautifully that God has shown us what is good and what He requires of us—to do justice, love mercy, and walk humbly. It's that simple.

I have a friend who struggles with a mental health issue. Before it manifested, he had accomplished some great things in the academic world and had been blessed with many honors. After graduation from a well-respected university, he held a high-paying job while also working on a master's degree from another prestigious, well-respected university. Then his life fell apart for several years while he struggled with his mental illness. Finally, he found medication that worked, and he began to pick up the pieces of his life.

He again found a job, but it had a much lower salary and was one that the world would not consider much of a job. Still, he went to work every day and did his best at this new job, which many with his level of intelligence and academic accomplishments would have considered below them. I watched as this wonderful young man learned to live a humble life. I found I admired him even more, knowing all he had been through and that instead of becoming bitter, he learned to do what Micah 6:8 describes as good. He learned to walk humbly.

Prayer: Heavenly Father, help us to see things through Your eyes. Help us to value what You value and to apply that to our own lives in the choices we make and the way we live. In Jesus' name, Amen.

Thought for the Day: What do you value? Who do you hold in high regard? Why?

Day 2: Finding Warmth in Winter

by Shirley
Read: Psalm 91:14-16

*Come to me, all who labor and are heavy
laden, and I will give you rest.*
Matthew 11:28

God created the seasons—yes, even winter—
for a purpose (Psalm 74:17). Winter is part of God's
plan for the world. There are things that I love about
each season and some things I don't like about each
one. In the winter, the air is usually crisp and cold,
clothing colors are rich, and the pace of life slows
down a bit, except during the holidays. Since days
are shorter in the winter, some find they leave home
for work in the morning when it is dark and arrive
back home from work when it is dark again.

In the darkness and cold of winter, most of us
try to find ways to keep warm. We put on layers of
warm clothing, coats, scarves, gloves, heavy socks,
boots, and hats. When we have been outside in the

cold for a period of time and come inside to find a warm place in our home, car, church, or office, we are grateful for the heat that warms our toes, hands, and nose.

The cold temperatures and fewer hours of sunshine usually send us inside for much of the time. Don't you just love to come inside from the cold, make a cup of hot tea or chocolate, sit in your favorite chair in front of a roaring fire in the fireplace, and read a good book?

During nature's winter, trees are bare, but not dead, for their roots are resting and waiting for their growth season in the spring. Similarly, our spiritual winter seasons allow God to work in our hearts to bring about transformation.

Sometimes our hurts, struggles, and trials take their toll on us and our hearts turn cold. We allow the stresses, worries, disappointments, and common trials to influence the choices we make that result in our hearts turning cold. We often feel disconnected from God, or like we are in a spiritually dry phase. We often feel all alone, as if God has abandoned us. We do not sense God's presence and we do not feel His love. Sometimes we begin feeling apathetic.

When we are experiencing these aspects of our spiritual winter, we need to take a close look at our relationship with Christ and make certain we have been diligent to transform our thinking by the continual renewing of our minds (Romans 12:2) and have daily put on the armor of God (Ephesians 6:10-18) so that our faith is strengthened and we can overcome the doubts and fears that creep in.

Some of you may be in a spiritual winter as you are reading this devotion. The first thing to remember is not to lose hope, for this season will not last forever. For those who are not currently in a spiritual winter, get ready and be alert, for a spiritual winter is certainly just around the corner. Prepare yourself.

These spiritual winters may be preparing us for longer and colder winters to come. Peter tells us that the trials prove that our faith is genuine (1 Peter 1:6-7). We need to ask forgiveness for our sins that have put distance between us and God. Be diligent to pray, even when it feels your prayers don't get above the ceiling. During a spiritual winter, we can choose to trust in God's control and loving care.

Take time to be still and rest in the assurance that God is in control and will forgive, guide, and protect you. Focus your thoughts on God and His truths in the Bible. You will begin to realize that His love, grace, and mercy is warming and thawing your cold heart.

Prayer: Gracious Father, we thank You for the spiritual winters we experience and for the time to slow down a little and refocus our hearts on You. Thank You for Your mercy, grace, love, and strength that keeps us warm! In the name of Jesus, Amen.

Thought for the Day: The coldness and separation that are sometimes part of spiritual winters do not last forever! Choose to trust in God and He will warm and thaw your cold heart.

Day 3: That Cold North Wind

by Harriet
Read: 1 John 5:3-5

*I have told you these things, so that in me
you may have peace.
In this world you will have trouble.
But take heart!
I have overcome the world.*
John 16:33 (NIV)

The North wind doth blow

And we shall have snow,

And what will poor robin do then,

> poor thing?

He'll sit in a barn

And keep himself warm

And hide his head under his wing,

> poor thing.

So goes the first verse of a British nursery
rhyme believed to have originated in the sixteenth
century. I learned this little verse as a child, and

even as a child in Africa, I remember it vividly. We had a little book of nursery rhymes with this verse in it and a picture of a brightly colored robin perched on a rafter inside a barn as seen through the barn door. Snow covered the ground and came down hard all around the outside of the barn.

The specifics about the origin of this little poem are not known, but its message is still clear—when the harsh winter weather comes, it's best to stay somewhere safe and warm while you wait out the storm.

Storms will come in our lives, too. I have certainly seen stormy days in my life, some that I have shared from time to time in articles or books, and others too personal to share publicly, but that left me storm-tossed and picking up pieces. What storms have you seen? Are you in the midst of a storm right now? The old poem's message is still sage advice.

Where is our safe spot when storms pelt our lives or our loved ones' lives? Where is the barn we can fly to and find refuge? Our refuge is God, through Jesus Christ. He alone can calm the seas that rage around us and part the waters that block us from crossing into our promised land. I am not talking about a name-it, claim-it kind of religion, either. Though God does sometimes miraculously resolve situations and knock down barriers, He also often holds our hands as we walk through the storms. He transcends the world and through Him we can transcend our circumstances, even as we face them.

I've heard it said that God lightens a person's load by either taking away all or some of the burden or by making the person carrying it stronger. In my life, more often than not, I've seen Him make the carrier stronger.

I started this devotion with robins, but I will end it with sparrows. Matthew 6:25-26 (NIV) says, "Therefore I tell you, do not worry about your life, what you will eat or drink; or about your body, what you will wear. Is not life more than food, and the body more than clothes? Look at the birds of the air; they do not sow or reap or store away in barns, and yet your heavenly Father feeds them. Are you not much more valuable than they?" And Matthew 10:29-31 (NIV) reminds us, "Are not two sparrows sold for a penny? Yet not one of them will fall to the ground outside your Father's care. And even the very hairs of your head are all numbered. So don't be afraid; you are worth more than many sparrows." As the words of an old hymn say, "His eye is on the sparrow, and I know He watches me."

Prayer: Gracious Father, You are our shelter from the storms of life and our refuge in them. When that cold north wind blows in our lives, help us to run to You and to hold on tightly. In Jesus' name, Amen.

Thought for the Day: "God is our refuge and strength, an ever-present help in trouble" (Psalm 46:1 NIV).

Day 4: Finding Joy in Winter

by Shirley
Read: James 1:2-8

*Count it all joy, my brothers, when you
meet trials of various kinds ...*
James 1:2a

Winter in Alabama means a great deal of rain. I do not like the combination of shorter days and rain, and often catch myself complaining about the weather and lack of daylight. However, I do love winter, particularly the crisp, cold air. I enjoy walking and looking at all the trees with no leaves. I find beauty in those gnarly limbs.

There are many comparisons we can make between nature's winter and our spiritual winter. When I am experiencing dark days of spiritual discipline, trials, or struggles, I often complain about what is going on and how unhappy I am. Sometimes I even complain about how unfair things in life are.

We know from the third chapter of Ecclesiastes that God establishes a time for everything that happens. When we are walking through a difficult situation, or spiritual winter, it is sometimes difficult to keep our heads above water and our hearts out of the pits of desperation. God knows that about us; after all, He created us. So, God made sure that the Bible included encouragement for His people who are deep in the throes of a trial.

There are so many who teach and preach that "If you just trust in Jesus, He will make everything okay." They often continue talking about the material blessings that will come your way. Sometimes, they even say if you send them a certain amount of money, God will take away your trial and bless you.

This is not true! The Bible does not promise us material blessings or that the trials in which we find ourselves will be removed. What it does promise is so much better—far above our ability to comprehend.

In today's passage, James tells us to "Count it all joy … when you meet trials of various kinds …" Huh? Experience joy in the midst of a trial? Note

James doesn't say "if" trials come, he says "when" they come.

James tells us there is a reason for the trials that come into our lives. "For you know that the testing of your faith produces steadfastness" (James 1:3). James continues by instructing us to, "Let steadfastness have its full effect, that you may be perfect and complete, lacking in nothing." Trials help strengthen our faith so that by God's grace and strength we can walk steadily through whatever happens.

You can do an internet search and find many definitions for joy. My definition, gleaned from my studies and the teaching of numerous folks through the years, is: A beautiful radiance that exudes from a Christ-follower who has absolute confidence in the Sovereign God in whom he or she places his or her security.

Does this mean that a Christ-following parent in the emergency room who just watched their teenager die from injuries in a car wreck walks out saying "Whoopee! My child died!" Absolutely not! Remember, God created our emotions and gave us the ability to love. We grieve, cry—sob uncontrollably—and sometimes it feels as though our hearts will break into a gazillion pieces.

So, what's the difference? A Christ-follower does not "grieve as others do who have no hope" (1 Thessalonians 4:13b). As we grieve, we place our faith, trust, and hope in God who will strengthen us and give us the grace to walk through any situation. In other words, the joy of the Lord will exude from us and others will see God's strength, grace, mercy, and love as He carries us through the situation.

Our ability to experience joy is directly related to our relationship with God. If sin is hindering our relationship with Him, we must be quick to confess and repent of that sin and walk in the freedom of our forgiveness with joy.

How are you finding joy in winter?

Prayer: Heavenly Father, thank You for not letting us walk through the trials in our lives without Your presence, love, strength, grace, and mercy. Help us learn to trust in You so that we are able to radiate that absolute confidence in You as we place our security in Your hands. In Jesus' name, Amen.

Thought for the Day: "May the God of hope fill you with all joy and peace in believing, so that by the power of the Holy Spirit you may abound in hope" (Romans 15:13).

Day 5: Through a Glass Darkly

by Harriet
Read: 1 Corinthians 13:9-13

For now we see through a glass darkly;
but then face to face:
now I know in part; but then shall I know
even as also I am known.
1 Corinthians 13:12 (KJV)

I scraped the frost off the bedroom window of my grandfather's old farmhouse. The ground sloped down from the back of the house, giving that window a panoramic view of the fields below. It had snowed the night before and I tried to see how things looked, but I couldn't quite tell. The frost on the other side of the window was too thick. I could only make out some things. I thought the sun was shining because I caught glimpses of blue skies through the frosted pane. The ground below glistened brightly too, so I knew the snow must have stopped. But that was about all I could make out.

My grandfather built his house with his own hands. This memory is from my childhood many years ago. Even back then, Granddaddy's house was the only place I remember ever seeing frost on the window so thick that it obscured the view. All other houses I have experienced since then have had double-paned, insulated windows which did not gather thick frost on them. At Granddaddy's the frost was sometimes even on the inside of the window.

A little while later, I put my coat, gloves, and boots on and stepped outside to a most spectacular view. It was a winter wonderland! Thick snow blanketed the ground and hung on the trees near the old farmhouse. The roof of the house was covered with snow, too. Everything looked white, clean, and beautiful. The sun hung like a yellow ball in the bluest of skies and its rays made the icy world sparkle. Now I could see everything clearly. Instead of straining to make out what was on the other side of a darkened window, now I could just open my eyes and look around.

I always think of this childhood memory when

I read today's passage, 1 Corinthians 13:9-13. It speaks of the fact that in our current life, with our finite, human minds, we are simply not able to comprehend everything there is to understand about God. He is vast and infinite and, according to Isaiah 55:8-9, His ways are not like our ways. His thoughts and ways are higher than our ways or understanding. And yet, someday when we shed this earthly body and this earthly dwelling, we will see Him face to face!

I think this is how we will feel when we see God face to face—like I felt that morning, so long ago when I strained to see the world outside my Grandfather's frosted window. But then, a few minutes later, I stepped outside and saw all things clearly.

In this life, we can only make out some of who God is. There is enough information in His word for us to have an understanding of Him if we study and work at it, but there are still lingering questions and things we cannot wrap our brains around. Someday, however, it will feel like stepping outside of the old farmhouse—we will clearly see God in all His beauty and wonder! What a glorious day that will be!

Prayer: Heavenly Father, how wonderful it will be to behold Your face! Until then, thank You for revealing Yourself to us through Your word. Help us to apply ourselves and become students of Your word. In Jesus' name, Amen.

Thought for the Day: Get excited that someday we will see God's face!

Chapter 11

Winter Waiting

Day 1: Waiting … Again!

by Shirley
Read: Isaiah 40:28-31

I wait for the LORD, my soul waits,
and in his word I hope;
My soul waits for the Lord more than
watchmen for the morning,
More than watchmen for the morning.
Psalm 130:5-6

I cannot think of a person I know whose favorite thing is waiting, can you? Waiting often feels like a colossal waste of time.

My memories of hospital waiting rooms evoke a myriad of emotions: sadness, grief, fear, thankfulness, and gratitude, to name a few. I've been in waiting rooms too many times to remember, but some of those situations I will never forget. I was there twice with my dad, first for open-heart surgery and again for a stroke. My mom had open-heart surgery too. And I was there when my nephew was badly burned. And so many times when friends were seriously injured or ill.

There are commonalities in a waiting room: out-of-date magazines, the sound of whispered conversations, someone pacing around the room, people hugging each other, and some praying. When a doctor enters the waiting room, everyone takes a deep breath in case he or she is there to deliver bad news about their loved one. When good news is delivered, family members cry tears of relief.

We all spend a good deal of time in waiting rooms. Some of those are actual waiting rooms at hospitals and doctors' offices. Then there are other waiting room situations—times of anxious waiting, uncertainty, questioning, overwhelming fear, and heartache.

Why is waiting so difficult for all of us? The answer will vary from person to person, yet often our problem with waiting is that we don't know what all is going on, we don't have all the details. We think we know how everything should proceed and we want God to proceed our way on our schedule, not His. When God doesn't move on our timeline, we sometimes end up being angry with God.

There are many biblical accounts of people who had to wait on God. Joseph is an excellent example. After his brother's sold him into slavery, he was unjustly thrown into jail. He continued to worship God, but he had to wonder how long he would be there, blamed for something he didn't do. There are others who experienced the frustration of waiting like Noah, Job,

Abraham, David, and the apostle Paul. Their lives help us see God's hand in the lives of these people and how He used their waiting periods to grow their faith, and they in turn help grow our faith.

God uses times of waiting to transform us more into His image. Waiting helps us develop patience. Waiting is part of the sanctification process whereby some of our sharp edges are buffed away. Waiting, particularly during difficulties, deepens our relationship with God as we lean on Him and trust Him to carry us through the situation. When you share waiting room experiences with a friend, those relationships often deepen and flourish (Proverbs 18:24).

What do we do while we wait? Here are a few things I have found helpful to do while in the waiting room:

- Trust in God's loving protective care.
- Be alert and pray for strength.
- Read, study, meditate and contemplate upon God's word.
- Be quick to confess and repent if the Holy Spirit convicts you of sin. It is important to note that waiting is not always the result of our sin.

Isaiah tells us, "But they who wait for the LORD

shall renew their strength; they shall mount up with wings like eagles; they shall run and not be weary; they shall walk and not faint" (Isaiah 40:31). Our ability to wait on the Lord is dependent upon the level of trust and confidence we have in Him.

Thank God He is always with us while we wait!

Prayer: Heavenly Father, help us trust You during the times when we are waiting. Help us look to You for the strength, grace, mercy, and patience to endure. In Jesus' name, Amen.

Thought for the Day: "The Lord is good to those who wait for him, to the soul who seeks him" (Lamentations 3:25).

Day 2: Tell it Not

by Harriet
Read: Isaiah 40:28-31

Tell it not in Gath,
proclaim it not in the streets of Ashkelon,
lest the daughters
of the Philistines be glad ...
2 Samuel 1:20 (NIV)

The words in our key verse, "Tell it not in Gath" were uttered by King David after he learned of Jonathan's death. David was grieved when he said these words. They were not actually a commandment to his troops as much as a wish that he knew could not come true. "Tell it not in Gath" was a proverb in those days that expressed a desire for one's enemies not to hear about calamity that the person had suffered. The phrase is first seen in Micah 1:10.

Some years ago, I studied Micah in an in-depth Bible study. What I learned about this verse, at that time, struck me as particularly poignant. The prophet Micah predicted an upcoming calamity upon the divided kingdom of Israel. Israel's enemies lived in Gath. Micah's words, "Tell it not in Gath," essentially meant, "Don't let our enemies know of our impending calamity because they will rejoice." This is sad to me. Micah was called by God to make a prophecy that he wished he did not have to make. Like every Israelite at the time, he especially didn't want his enemies to know, and so he mouthed the wish that it not be told in Gath—the home of his enemy.

My brother-in-law used to jokingly say, "Don't tell people your problems because half of them don't care and the other half are glad you have them."

This chapter is titled "Winter Waiting" because winter is a time when nothing grows as the world lies dormant waiting for spring. It could be seen as a time of disappointment and discouragement waiting for forward movement in one's life or agenda. It is a long sequence of short days and long nights when nothing grows.

Have you ever had times of disappointment when things happened to you or to someone you loved, that you hoped people outside your trusted few would not learn of? I've been there more times than I want to remember.

But take heart. Our focal passage today from Isaiah 40 helps us see these times of disappointment and waiting from God's perspective. This passage tells us that He is the everlasting God who does not grow tired or weary and that He gives strength to the weary and increases the power of the weak. And then comes that wonderful passage so many of us have committed to memory, Isaiah 40:31. The New International Version of the Bible puts it this way, "But those who hope in the LORD will renew their strength. They will soar on wings like eagles; they will run and not grow weary, they will walk and not be faint."

We can tell God about our problems. He cares. He is with us in this time of disappointment and waiting. And just like spring flowers, in His perfect timing, our lives will be renewed and alive with freshness of faith and purpose once again.

Prayer: Heavenly Father, waiting can be so difficult, and disappointments hard to bear. Hold us in Your arms during challenging times in our lives. Keep us in the warmth of Your love during seasons in our lives that feel long and cold. Help us to keep our eyes on You. In Jesus' name, Amen.

Thought for the Day: Nothing surprises God. He knows what you are going through and is walking beside you through it.

Day 3: Not What I Had in Mind

by Shirley
Read: Isaiah 55:6-9

For my thoughts are not your thoughts
neither are your ways my ways,
declares the LORD.
For as the heavens are higher
than the earth,
so are my ways higher than your ways
and my thoughts than your thoughts.
Isaiah 55:8-9

Some time ago, I was spending several hours with a friend of mine who has early-onset Alzheimer's disease. I met her at the salon where she was having her hair done. After the appointment, we got settled into my car to go to a Bible study together and eat lunch. I put the key in the ignition and turned it—nothing! "Really God?" I thought as I breathed a quick prayer, "Lord, please make my car start!" Tried again—nothing!

I told my friend the battery seemed dead and that I would call for help. I grabbed my phone and called AAA. I reported that my battery was dead and gave the address where they could find us and reported that we were in a safe place.

I explained to my friend that help was on the way but that it might take as long as thirty minutes for help to arrive, all the time praying that help would arrive quickly. I suggested we go ahead and start our Bible study. I grabbed my Bible and the book we were using for our Bible study discussions: *Study Guide on Prayer—A Companion to Prayer: It's Not About You.*

When we opened the study guide to the place we left off at our last study, I asked her to read the question at the top of the page. She began reading aloud, "God's plans are not our plans. They often do not fit our ideas of how things should go."

She looked up at me and said, "That's right!"

I said, "He always knows what's best, doesn't He? Even if I don't like having a dead battery, that is God's plan for us right now!" And, I whispered a prayer asking the Lord to help me trust His plan and timing.

I then started to recall all of the things in this situation for which we could be thankful: "It is daylight, we are in a safe place, help is on the way, God is with us …" I stopped for a breath.

My friend added, "And I'm here."

Just about then a mechanic arrived, and in no time the car started. The battery was seven years old, so since the man had a battery with him, I had him go ahead and replace it for me.

We covered another study question while he installed the battery and got the car going. As we drove to the restaurant I continued talking about God's plans and my plans often not being the same.

All of this occurred in about twenty-five minutes or so. Admittedly, until my friend read that question, my mind had not been filled with thankfulness. Instead, I was trying to stay calm and think of ways to ensure that my friend felt safe.

Although my first reaction was to question God, I know that God was right there with us and that He enabled me to stay calm and help focus my friend's attention on our Bible study. It is during situations like this that the Lord graciously transforms my thinking so that I don't view the circumstance as negative.

I've learned to ask the Lord, "What do I need

to learn in this situation?" Sometimes, through the prompting of the Holy Spirit, I discover a sin for which I need to confess and repent. Other times, I realize I need to focus my thoughts on God and His character, or that I need to slow down, or some other thing. This time, I simply needed to trust God and thank Him for His protection and provision—regardless!

As Christ-followers we are to trust God and His will for us, as our key passage tells us. So, even when God's plans are not what I had in mind, I know everything that happens is part of God's plan to sanctify me—to make me more like Him.

Prayer: Our gracious Heavenly Father, thank You for Your direction, provision, and protection during those times that Your plans are not our plans. Bring to mind the things for which we can be thankful and give us the clarity of mind to follow Your leading. In the name of Your Son Jesus, Amen.

Thought for the Day: When God's plans are not what you had in mind, thank Him for His direction, provision, and protection that enables you to trust

Him as you walk through the fulfillment of His plan.

Day 4: Keeping Busy

by Harriet
Read: Luke 4:38-42

Sitting down,
Jesus called the Twelve and said,
"Anyone who wants to be first
must be the very last,
and the servant of all."
Mark 9:35 (NIV)

"Don't just stand there. Do something!"

So, it's a long, cold, slow, boring winter, huh? Well, as my mother would always say, "Find something constructive to do." I can almost hear her voice in my ears now, saying those words. The cold air won't let you stand still for long, anyway.

The fourth chapter of Luke tells a very short story of a miraculous healing. "Now Simon's mother-in-law was suffering from a high fever, and they asked Jesus to help her. So he bent over her and rebuked the fever, and it left her. She got up at once and began to wait on them" (Luke 4:38-39

NIV).

When I came across these verses in my personal devotions, it was not the healing of Simon's mother-in-law that struck me as unusual, though it certainly was. All of Jesus' miraculous healings were unusual and amazing, but because I have heard and read them many times over the years, they seem quite familiar. What was not familiar to me in this passage was Simon's mother-in-law's actions after she was healed.

What did she do in response to her miraculous healing at the hands of the Messiah? Did she hire a publicist and get personal recognition for it? Did she make a speech in order to get even her fifteen minutes of fame? No. Well then, did she retire to her bedroom and take it easy? After all, she had been very sick. Again, no. It says she immediately arose and waited on them. Wow. She hopped up from her illness and started helping others.

When I think of lending a hand to others, I remember when my grandson visited me when he was just a little boy. As he stood in front of the open pantry with his little arms lifted up, my then three-year-old grandson, Grason, asked me for help.

"Lala, can you help me? I can't reach the snacks, and I want to get some popcorn for Ty."

Thirteen-year-old Ty, Grason's uncle and my son, had just walked into the kitchen complaining of hunger. The popcorn was on a shelf too high for a small boy to reach, but it was not too high for a teenager. Ty could have reached the popcorn himself, but instead, I lifted Grason up to the shelf to get the popcorn. After retrieving the popcorn, I lifted Grason up to the microwave and helped him push the buttons, so it would pop. Grason was so proud as he handed his uncle that freshly popped popcorn.

Who was helping whom? Was Grason helping Ty, or was I helping Grason … or maybe Ty? It occurred to me God's economy is sort of like that. He asks us to help each other, to bear each other's burdens, as it says in Galatians 6:2. The early church is described in Acts 2:45 as sharing with each other according to each one's need. Are we practicing those principles in our lives today? There is always a job that needs to be done in God's economy even if you are stuck at home during these cold winter days. Cards of encouragement can be written from home. Food can be prepared to share with others later. Lesson plans worked on for whatever group God has given to you as a ministry, and so much more. I pray we will all become like children, eagerly desiring to help another while at the same time unashamed to ask for help when we need it.

Prayer: Heavenly Father, give us willing hearts to help our brothers and sisters in need. Thank You for teaching these practices in Your word. Fill our time with things to do for Your kingdom. In Jesus' name, Amen.

Thought for the Day: There's plenty to be done— better get busy.

Day 5: Kept by the Power of God

by Shirley
Read: 1 Peter 1:3-8

Who are kept
by the power of God through faith
for salvation ready to be revealed
in the last time.
1 Peter 1:5 (NKJV)

One precious lady I knew when I was in my early teens, Mama G, impressed upon me that we are "kept by the power of God," as she would say. Mom took me with her to visit Mama G after she had a debilitating stroke. I was a little afraid to go into the nursing home room because I wasn't sure how badly the stroke affected her. I kept behind Mom and kind of peeked around her to see what Mama G looked like after having a stroke. I was very surprised to see her sitting up in the hospital bed. When she saw Mom at the door, she flashed a huge—and very crooked—smile.

Mom pulled me from behind her so Mama G

could see me. Mom made a joke about the fact that I had been talking incessantly until just then. Mama G motioned for me to come a little closer. When I was standing close by, she half sang, and half mumbled, "We are kept by the power of God." Mom immediately recognized the old hymn and began singing the chorus with her. Admittedly, I was in a little bit of shock at the sight of Mama G and too embarrassed by my mom's singing to pay attention to the words, but Mom took time to explain them to me a little later as we traveled home.

Do you know this hymn, "Kept by the Power of God" by Barney E. Warren? It is based on today's passage. If you are not familiar with it, look it up online. The chorus says:

> We are kept by the power of God,
> We are kept by the power of God;
> By trusting, obeying,
> By watching and praying,
> We are kept by the power of God.

Through the years I have thought long and hard

about this passage of Scripture and hymn. I couldn't figure out why we had to do stuff (trust, obey, watch, pray) if God's power was keeping us.

I now understand the answer is that God is 100% sovereign and powerful and I am 100% responsible to be obedient to His commands to trust, obey, watch, and pray. There is so much rich biblical truth in the verses of this hymn.

The first verse reminds us that since we are being "kept by the power and favor of God," sin does not rule us anymore (Romans 6:14) because He lives within us (Ephesians 3:17) and because we are cleansed by His blood (1 John 1:9).

Verse two reminds us that we are being "kept by the power of God through faith" as long as we "walk in the light" (1 John 1:7) with Jesus who is always with us (Matthew 28:20).

Verse three reminds us we are being "kept by the power of God if we trust" and we will not get weary (Isaiah 40:31).

Verse four reminds us that we are being "kept by the power of God each day." As a result, we will tell of Him over and over (Psalm 89:1). We will also be conquerors through Him (Romans 8:37) and defeat every enemy or evil thing that comes our way (1 John 3:8).

When you think of all these things about being kept by the power of God, what comes to your mind? Are you thinking about what God has done for you in the past when He gave you new life in Him? I certainly hope so! Are you thinking about what God is going to do for you in the future when you receive your inheritance of eternal life? I certainly hope so! These are the things I seem to focus on the most.

Yet it is important to remember another important truth. Right now, God is at work helping you deal with the pressures, weariness, frustrations, suffering, temptations, anxieties, fears, and so on. Do not miss this important truth that God uses His divine power to protect us for our eternal salvation by sustaining our faith while we are here on earth.

Prayer: Powerful God, thank You that we do not have to depend upon ourselves to get good enough for salvation. Thank You for Your grace that secures our salvation in the past, present, and future. In Jesus' name, Amen.

Thought for the Day: We are kept by the power of God through faith.

Chapter 12

Renewal

Day 1: Beneath the Snow

by Harriet
Read: Titus 3:3-7

Restore us to yourself, LORD, that we
may return; renew our days as of old ...
Lamentations 5:21 (NIV)

Beneath the bitter cold snow, which covers the ground in the wintertime, are seeds that will grow and bud when the warm spring sun thaws the ground. Beautiful flowers will then burst forth from these seeds. With the changing of the season and the warming of the temperatures, the world will be renewed. Barren grounds and trees will again bring forth their foliage and appear lush and full.

For the world around us, winter is a time of renewal that is happening in ways we cannot see, but it is happening just the same. Renewal is defined as a replacing or repairing of something that has been worn down. Though we cannot see it, during late winter, the seeds and roots of plants that wore out and died the year before are being renewed and strengthened, making them ready to burst forth at the right time.

Spiritual renewal is defined as a renewal that occurs in a person's soul, heart, and mind rather than in one's body. We can have a spiritual renewal even if our bodies are aging, sick or in pain. Paul makes this point in 2 Corinthians 4:16 (NIV): "Though outwardly we are wasting away, yet inwardly we are being renewed day by day."

Winter days can seem long and boring. There is less daylight, so we spend more time indoors. Sometimes we get snowed in. I tend to go to bed a little earlier in the winter. In the summertime, I am sometimes just getting inside at nine o'clock when it finally turns dark, but in the winter, by the time nine o'clock gets here it has been dark for hours and I am about ready to go to bed.

God can use the long winter indoor times as a special time of spiritual renewal for us if we let him. What are you doing to carve out ways to allow God the opportunity to renew you? Are you attending a winter Bible study, getting involved in a mission activity of some kind, or just spending more time with God in your own devotions?

Romans 12:2 says some pretty amazing things about what happens if we allow God to renew our minds. It says, "Do not conform to the pattern of this world, but be transformed by the renewing of your mind. Then you will be able to test and approve what God's will is—his good, pleasing and perfect will." Did you get that? Allowing God to renew our minds through Bible study and prayer transforms us, making us into people who will do God's good and perfect will!

Flower seeds lie beneath the ice and snow ready to spring forth—what lies inside of you that God is shaping and preparing so that it too will spring forth in accordance to His will?

God shaped a writer inside of me—one I didn't know was there. He brought it out through a difficult time in my life. He squeezed it out of me through adversity. Like the flowers that bloom in the spring, this aspect of me was shaped in cold, icy times in my life. What lies beneath the snow in your life?

Prayer: Renew us, oh Lord! Shape our hearts and

minds in accordance with Your good and perfect will. In Your Son's name, Amen.

Thought for the Day: Beneath the snow lies a flower. What lies inside of you waiting for God to bring it forth?

Day 2: Are You Weary?

by Shirley
Read: Galatians 6:6-10

*And let us not grow weary of doing good,
for in due season we will reap,
if we do not give up.*
Galatians 6:9

Winter is one of my four favorite seasons. Okay, you got me, there are things that I love about each of the seasons. Winter is great because it is cold, and I love the cold. Granted, as I age, my bones and joints like the cold less and less.

As winter lingers on and on, I do get a little weary of the long, dreary days of little sunshine and in Alabama, a lot of rain. A drudgery of sort seems to settle upon me, and it takes concerted effort on my part to motivate myself to do anything.

When I am weary and want to talk things through with someone, I really miss my mom. For the last several years of her life, it was my privilege to live with her. She was such an example of someone whose faith in God was deeply rooted. We would talk about certain situations in which I needed to make a decision, and she would sing her response, "Tell it to Jesus, tell it to Jesus." I must confess at times I wanted to say, "I want to tell you, not Jesus," even though I knew she was right.

Do you know the hymn, "Tell It to Jesus"? Edmund S. Lorenz wrote the words in German and Jeremiah E. Rankin translated them into English. Each verse of this hymn asks two questions. Presuming a *yes* answer, the hymn asks, are you weary, heavyhearted, grieving over joys departed, crying uncontrollably, savoring hidden sin, fearing the coming storm, anxious about tomorrow? "Tell it to Jesus."

What a great reminder for all of us that regardless of how weary we are of the weather, a person, or a situation, and so on, we are to tell Jesus our thoughts, concerns, and feelings.

Of course, my mind immediately goes to the third verse of one of my many favorite hymns, "What a Friend We Have in Jesus," by Joseph M. Scriven:

Are we weak and heavy laden,
Cumbered with a load of care?
Precious Savior, still our refuge,
Take it to the Lord in prayer!

These hymns point to God who answers prayer. But let's back up a little bit. God is able to answer our prayers because He is God. That might seem a bit obvious, but it is foundational to His capability to answer our prayers.

Next, we need to remember that all of God's promises for answering prayers point to those prayers which are in line with His will. I think back over prayers I have prayed in the past and see that, thankfully, God answered them according to His will and not what I wanted. I can see His hand of protection and guidance through His answers, even when He has answered *no*.

Remember, God sees the whole picture, how our one request fits into His plan for us and everyone else. I have struggled with God when He answered some prayers differently from what I wanted. Those times of telling it to Jesus eventually resulted in me asking His forgiveness for not trusting Him!

These hymns point to many biblical truths about God. Among those truths are:

- He is our source of strength (Psalm 105:4).
- He is approachable and will help us when we need Him (Hebrews 4:16).
- He will sustain us (Psalm 55:22).
- He will give us rest (Matthew 11:28).

When you are weary, take your weariness and concerns to your Heavenly Father, who is able and willing to help you.

Prayer: Gracious Heavenly Father, thank You for the privilege You have given to Your children to talk with You about everything that is going on with us. Help us know You better so that we trust and rest in Your sovereign plan for our lives. In Jesus' name, Amen.

Thought for the Day: "God is our refuge and strength, a very present help in trouble" (Psalm 46:1).

Day 3: Just an Ordinary Person

by Harriet
Read: Acts 4:13-16

*Now as they observed
the confidence of Peter and John
and understood that they were
uneducated and untrained men,
they were amazed, and began to recognize
them as having been with Jesus.*
Acts 4:13 (NASB)

Peter and John were just ordinary people. They were uneducated and untrained, yet something transformed them, making them different from who they once were. It transformed them from ordinary to extraordinary. This transformation was so noticeable it caused those around them to marvel. What made the difference in them? They had been made new because they had been with Jesus!

Do we have that kind of difference about us? Can spending time with Jesus transform and renew us too? Can others tell that we have been with Jesus?

The pastor of the church I attended while growing up in Nigeria was just an ordinary man who had once been just an ordinary boy … until the day he heard about Jesus. When he accepted Christ as his Savior at the Christian school he attended, his family disowned him. In fact, they told him they would kill him if he did not renounce his new-found faith. Afraid for his life, Reverend Akinyleye escaped through a window in the middle of the night and ran away from home.

What gave him the confidence to risk his life and abandon his family rather than renounce his faith? He had been with Jesus. He was different. Romans 12:2 calls it being transformed by the renewing of our minds.

Bud was a similar man—as ordinary as apple pie until he had an encounter with God. My knowledge of Bud began when my husband, John, received a phone call from his friend, Brian.

"A man named Bud will be calling you to ask about becoming a Christian."

With these words, John's friend Brian began explaining a strange situation. Brian was a lay pastor at an inner-city church until he moved to another state after getting married. When Brian wasn't pastoring, he owned a small lawn company. Because he lived in an apartment above the church, he had kept some of his lawn equipment stored on a vacant lot next to the church.

Bud was a housing inspector for government housing and property, which the vacant lot happened to be. He called Brian to ask about the equipment that had not yet been moved, but after learning Brian was a pastor, Bud told him of a Bible he had also found in an apartment he was cleaning. Bud said, "I usually throw out the things I find when I inspect places, but this was a Bible, and you know, you just can't throw away a Bible. So, I started to read it, but I do not understand it at all."

Brian explained that he no longer lived in town. He gave Bud John's name and phone number as someone who could follow up with him and explain the Bible to him. Thus, began my husband's ministry with Bud, a man with a checkered background. Bud was a man who was dead in trespasses and sins; a child of wrath. He would have died that way ... but God placed a Bible in an abandoned government apartment. And Bud learned about Jesus and became a transformed man.

A few months later we had the privilege of attending Bud's baptism. He and John still stay in touch. Bud did not go on to change the world for Christ by having a world-renowned ministry of some kind. No, instead Christ changed Bud's world and that is extraordinary. These were all ordinary men—Peter and John of the Bible, Rev. Akinleye, Brian, my husband John, and Bud. Yet, God did an extraordinary thing in their lives. He saved their souls for all eternity and changed their lives on earth in a way that others noted, and by which they were impacted.

In these ordinary winter days, as we bundle up and face our daily activities, may we spend enough time with Jesus that others in our lives will notice a difference in us too!

Prayer: Heavenly Father, You call us to spend time with You and when we do, You change our lives. You make the ordinary extraordinary. Thank You. Amen.

Thought for the Day: Jesus makes all the

difference. How can you make Him more of a priority in your life?

Day 4: Do You Need Refinishing?

by Shirley
Read: Ecclesiastes 3:1-11a

He has made everything beautiful
in its time.
Ecclesiastes 3:11a

I grew up in a family of antique lovers and collectors. Okay, some of the things collected were more junk-tique than antique, but we collected them anyway.

Someone gave my daddy an antique washstand that had been passed down through a couple of generations of their family. By the time my dad got it, it had a good number of dings and scars though it was once covered in white enamel paint. On one of the back legs the white paint was chipped off and underneath you could see a layer of blue, one of green, and then a gross looking dark varnish.

My dad began the weeklong arduous task of refinishing the washstand. He had to take the doors and wheels off and remove the mirror and the mirror stand that sat on the top of the chest-like bottom piece. Then he used a stripper solution to soften the layers of paint and varnish so he could scrape them off. After that, he would reapply the stripper solution and scrape some more. He repeated this process several more times. Then he used a scouring pad and more stripper solution to remove the last bits of paint residue. The wood looked worn and in need of tender loving care. Next, he cleaned the wood with mineral spirits and then gently sanded the surfaces until they were all smooth.

At this point, he had to remove some old nails that had been hammered improperly and sand down a few sharp edges where little pieces of wood had broken off. Then he wiped it all down again with mineral spirits. After it dried, he ran his fingers across every square inch of wood to make sure it was all smooth. If he found a rough spot, he would gently sand it down and clean it with mineral spirits and let it dry.

When all of the wood passed Dad's smoothness tests, he gently covered it with sheets and left it for a day. The next day he carefully uncovered the pieces and did another smoothness check. When the pieces all passed a final smoothness check he began applying the varnish. He used a small brush at first and applied varnish in the corners and at the places where two different pieces met. Then he used a larger brush to apply the stain to the larger areas using long strokes.

The piece would be protected with sheets—not daring to let them touch the wet varnish—to dry overnight. The next morning, Dad would carefully inspect the piece for consistency in the layer of varnish and do a smoothness test again.

The good news is that the first coat of varnish passed all the inspections, so he applied a second coat. The piece was protected with sheets again and left to dry overnight.

When we did the great unveiling the next day all of the pieces looked great. The grain of the refinished oak was beautiful, yet the washstand was still in several pieces.

I had to run an errand for my mom while Dad began to carefully assemble all the pieces, putting the mirror back together and attaching it to the bottom chest. Then he attached the wheels which he had cleaned and polished.

When I got back home, I could not believe the refinished piece was the same old enamel white-painted washstand. It was beautiful and has served me very well in the years since it came to live in my home.

When I came to Christ my life looked a lot like that old washstand did when Dad first got it: dings and battle scars from my sin, and coat after coat of paint I applied trying to cover it up and make myself look clean.

The moment I became a Christ-follower, God began the work of sanctification (making me like Him) in my life. His sanctification has included softening my hardened heart and scraping away my sinful thoughts, habits, and desires. I'd like to say I am way past that stage to where there are just a few rough spots to smooth out, but thank God, He is still working to refinish (transform) me into a fully sanctified person who will enter God's kingdom as glorification (a new imperishable, spiritual body) takes place.

Are you in need of the Master Refinisher's

touch?

Prayer: Gracious Heavenly Father, we are in awe that You can take our horribly sinful and broken-down life and infuse it with Your loving refinishing touch to bring out beauty in us. Give us patience as You strip and sand away all the rough sinful edges. Thank You that You do not throw us away, but that You make us useful for the advancement of Your kingdom while we live on this earth and worthy of worshiping You for eternity in heaven. In Jesus' name, Amen.

Thought for the Day: God can take the ugliest and most sinful life and make it useful and beautiful for His work here on earth and for eternity.

Day 5: The Power of a Word

by Harriet
Read: Romans 15:18-21

*It has always been my ambition
to preach the gospel where Christ
was not known ...*
Romans 15:20 (NIV)

I once heard a story about Phil Tuttle, the president of Walk Thru the Bible. He told of an experience he had while talking to a Nigerian pastor. Naturally, this story caught my ear because of the connection I have with Nigeria. The man in the story asked Phil how he had become a pastor. Phil told the man all about his education—college, graduate school, seminary—along with various other types of training he had undergone in order to become a pastor. Then Phil asked the Nigerian how he became a pastor and was surprised and a bit amused at the man's answer. The man replied, "I had the loudest voice in the village."

Words are an interesting thing. They can be

ugly and mean, causing anger and hate. They can be silly and nonsensical. When I was a child, we had an African gray talking parrot who said some of the funniest, most nonsensical things! I can remember how hard he worked at saying, "supercalifragilisticexpialidocious," the silly word spoken in the movie, *Mary Poppins*. We all used to laugh at his efforts.

But words can also bring good news like they do when we share the gospel with others. When God created the world, He did it by speaking words, according to the book of Genesis. For instance, in the creation story found in Genesis 2, God said, "Let there be light," and there was light. "Let the dry land appear," and it appeared, and so forth.

This same miracle happens when we speak God's word to unbelievers. God again brings about a new creation through His word. 2 Corinthians 5:17 tells us that if anyone is in Christ, he is a new creature. The New International Version puts it this way, "Therefore, if anyone is in Christ, the new creation has come: The old has gone, the new is here!"

How does God speak His words to

unbelievers? He does it when His words, as recorded in the Bible, are read or professed aloud to others. God is still in the business of renewal through His Spirit and His word. He makes new creations through His word every day and the amazing thing is, He uses all who are willing to help in that work. These words can renew us and make new creatures out of us too if we meditate on them. In 2 Timothy 4:2 (NIV), we're encouraged to "preach the word; be prepared in season and out of season; correct, rebuke and encourage—with great patience and careful instruction."

In Hebrews, we read this about God's word: "For the word of God is alive and active. Sharper than any double-edged sword, it penetrates even to dividing soul and spirit, joints and marrow; it judges the thoughts and attitudes of the heart" (Hebrews 4:12 NIV).

We don't need a college education, graduate school, seminary degree, or any kind of special training to share the gospel with others. Though these things are good and helpful, they are not necessary. What is needed is a willing heart and, well, maybe the loudest voice in the village.

Prayer: Gracious Heavenly Father, thank You for Your life-changing word and the new creation that You make when someone hears the gospel and accepts it. Make us eager to share the good news with others! In Your Son's name, Amen.

Thought for the Day: Participate in God's creative miracle today. Speak His gospel to another in your most eager voice, if not your loudest!

Chapter 13

Here Comes Spring!

Day 1: Yearning for Sunshine

by Harriet
Read: Psalm 42:1-2, 113:3

*He is the radiance of the glory of God and
the exact imprint of his nature,
and he upholds the universe
by the word of his power.
After making purification for sins,
he sat down at the right hand of the
Majesty on high ...*
Hebrews 1:3

"Sun-lover." You are probably familiar with that term. It's often used for a person who is constantly trying to get their skin tan, or tanner as is often the case. These days people who long for a darker tan sometimes go to tanning booths, but back when I was a teenager, we slathered our bodies with baby oil and sat for hours in the sun. Thank goodness I never enjoyed that activity, and when my friends did it, I usually did not participate. But I did love the sun! I have always loved a bright, sunny day.

Growing up in Nigeria, I spent my childhood days playing in the tropical sun. There is nothing quite as beautiful as a bright blue African sky with a huge yellow ball in it and a few clouds floating by. In the rainy season, when the trees are full of foliage, the sunlight streaks through them casting specks of sunshine on the ground that dances as the wind blows. How I loved the speckled sunshine of my childhood!

This time of year, when the long winter is nearly over, and spring is just around the corner, I savor the warmth of the sun! The days grow longer, and outside tasks begin to beckon me. After all, I have just come through a long string of cold, short, dreary days, and those are hard on the little African child who still dwells inside of me.

In our key verse, Jesus is described as radiant. Like the radiant sun, He warms us with His love and causes us to bloom and grow like flowers. But do we long for Him the way we long for the sun this time of year? I am asking myself that question—do I long for Jesus as much as I long for the sun on cold winter days?

Psalm 42:1-2 (NIV) puts it another way. It

says, "As the deer pants for streams of water, so my soul pants for you, my God. My soul thirsts for God, for the living God."

I know what it feels like to be extremely thirsty. As a child, my friends and I could only drink from the faucets in the kitchens of our mission houses because those faucets had filters on them. None of the other faucets in other places or outside had a filter. We could use that water to wash our hands, bodies or clothes, or to water our gardens, but we could not drink water from those faucets. I have had many afternoons of play under that tropical sun when I did not want to go back home to the one faucet I knew was safe, so I played on and grew ever more thirsty as the day wore on. By the time the sun went down, and I returned home, I was so thirsty! I do not ever remember being that thirsty in America.

So I have to ask myself, do I thirst for God like that? Do I run to my Bible to study His word like I used to run into the kitchen to get a drink of water? Do I eagerly lap up new understandings of God's word the way I lapped up water as a child? I can remember drinking as fast as I could swallow and feeling like I couldn't get enough. Do I do that with God's word?

Do you? Do you worship God the way some seem to worship the sun? Do you soak up His teachings like someone trying to get a tan soaks up the sun?

Prayer: Heavenly Father, shine warmly on us today. Fill us with a yearning for You as we go about our day. May we find ourselves thirsting for You. Prick our hearts that we will long to turn them toward You like a flower longs to turn toward the sunshine in the springtime. In Jesus' name, Amen.

Thought for the Day: Do you thirst for God as much as you would thirst for a drink of water when parched? What steps can you take to draw closer to Him and feel more of the warmth of His presence flooding into your life?

Day 2: To Crumble and Prepare

by Shirley
Read: Isaiah 28:23-26

*Sow righteousness for yourselves, reap
the fruit of unfailing love,
and break up your unplowed ground; for
it is time to seek the LORD,
until he comes and showers his
righteousness on you.*
Hosea 10:12 (NIV)

With the arrival of winter's cold weather, things can get a little gloomy. There are fewer hours of sunshine, if the sun shines at all. The ground gets cold and hard—I know from all the times I have fallen and hit that cold and hard ground. Leaves fall off the trees and things appear dead. Of course, we know from science that the trees aren't dead when the leaves fall off and the grass isn't dead just because the ground is cold and hard. The trees, grass, and ground are resting and preparing for their season of growth that starts in the spring.

With the first glimpse of a daffodil I'm ready

for spring to begin, aren't you? The cold and dreary days of winter begin to wear on me and I'm ready for a change. I'm that way with every season—I'm excited for it to begin and get tired of it after a while. But I realize that God created each season to serve a purpose on earth, just like the seasons serve a purpose in our spiritual lives.

There is a hymn that is not very well known nowadays: "As From the Winter Sky." James Montgomery wrote verses that talk about the seasons. It gives an interesting perspective about the purpose of winter—on earth and in our spiritual lives.

As from the winter sky,
When keen the tempests blow,
O'er fields that waste and barren lie,
Descends the softening snow;

Not with ice-binding cold
To chill the stubborn soil,
But crumble and prepare the mould
To meet the plougher's toil.

I love the imagery here! The snow doesn't fall to further chill the already cold and hardened ground; snow falls to help crumble and prepare the ground for ploughing and planting in the spring.

That puts a little different perspective on the spiritual seasons in our spiritual life also, doesn't it? The times when we feel the coldness cutting through our hearts, the cold damp snow gathering to smother them, they are actually accomplishing just the opposite. They are helping to crumble our resistance and prepare our hearts for the planting and growth seasons.

Sometimes the hardness and coldness of our hearts is the result of unconfessed sin. Sometimes it is because we are smothering under the weight of the burdens we are carrying by ourselves.

During these times when our hearts are cold to spiritual matters, we feel as though we are smothering from the weight of burdens like so many coats and blankets trying to warm us back into fellowship with God. Those "burdens"—circumstances of life around us—serve a purpose to soften our hearts so that we are sensitive to the prompting of the Holy Spirit as He convicts, encourages, and strengthens our faith.

> "And I will give you a new heart, and a
> new spirit I will put within you. And I will
> remove the heart of stone from your flesh
> and give you a heart of flesh. And I will
> put my Spirit within you, and cause you to
> walk in my statutes and be careful to obey
> my rules" (Ezekiel 36:26-27).

The prophet Ezekiel wrote these verses to the children of Israel during the Babylonian captivity, so they were a promise to a specific people at a specific time. However, when we look at other places in Scripture, we see similar promises that when Christ redeems us, we become a new creation. 2 Corinthians 5:17 is one example: "Therefore, if anyone is in Christ, he is a new creation. The old has passed away; behold, the new has come."

Prayer: Our gracious Heavenly Father, we thank You for loving us enough to send the cold winds and snow into our lives so that our hardened hearts are softened and sensitive to the prompting of Your Holy Spirit. Thank You that Your word will bear fruit in and through our lives. In Jesus' name, Amen.

Thought for the Day: God lovingly crumbles and prepares our hearts for the plowing, planting, and growth in our future.

Day 3: No Winter Lasts Forever

by Harriet
Read: Genesis 8:18-22

Because of the LORD's great love
we are not consumed,
for his compassions never fail.
They are new every morning;
great is your faithfulness.
Lamentations 3:22-23 (NIV)

"Always winter but never Christmas." Most of us are familiar with this quote from C. S. Lewis's book, *The Lion, the Witch, and the Wardrobe.* According to the story, this was the condition of the land of Narnia when the children first arrived. A wicked witch had cast a cold spell on Narnia, freezing it and making it always winter, but never Christmas.

This may make a good setting and plotline for a fantasy book such as the ones Lewis wrote when he wrote *The Chronicles of Narnia,* but fortunately, it is not our situation, because our God is a faithful

God. In our key passage today, we read where Noah praises God, declaring that as long as the earth exists it will continue to cycle the way we now know it to do, causing the seasons to change in a regular pattern. In tropical lands, like where I grew up, the rainy season will always follow the dry season and the earth will again bear fruit. In colder climates like we have in America, spring will surely follow winter … always!

God is faithful in more than just the seasons of the earth. He is faithful in our lives, too. Sometimes the winters we experience are symbolic winters— long periods of time when we face difficulties or even painful situations in our lives. Hang in there; no winter lasts forever because ours is a faithful God.

A favorite passage of mine speaks this truth when it says, "I would have despaired unless I had believed that I would see the goodness of the LORD in the land of the living. Wait for the LORD; be strong and let your heart take courage; yes, wait for the LORD" (Psalm 27:13-14 NASB).

In Narnia, the spell was finally broken by Aslan, the true king, and their snow finally started melting. C.S. Lewis may have had his own conversion experience in mind when he wrote about the freezing of Narnia in *The Lion, the Witch, and the Wardrobe.* He described his conversion in his book, *Surprised by Joy: The Shape of My Early Life,* saying that he felt like a man of snow who was finally beginning to melt.

I have had symbolic winters in my life. I remember going through difficult times two autumns in a row. I had always liked the fall season and I usually decorated my house with autumn decorations, but for the next couple of years after the two traumatic years, when autumn came around, my heart sank, and I did not feel like decorating. Then one year, without even thinking about the difficult experiences of a few years prior, I pulled out my fall decorations and started putting them up. That's when it hit me—God had healed my hurting heart and given me joy again. He had melted the snows in my heart and brought my symbolic winter to an end.

As it says in Psalm 119:90 (NIV), "Your faithfulness continues through all generations; you established the earth, and it endures." Spring will

come again, this year and every year thereafter until
the Lord returns to take us home.

Prayer: Great is Your faithfulness, oh Lord. Thank
You! Help us in the winters we must face, whether
they be literal or symbolic. In Jesus' name, Amen.

Thought for the Day: The snow is melting. Spring
is coming! Look for details of God in the changes
you see in the world around you.

Day 4: Cling to Hope

by Shirley
Read: Hebrews 10:19-25

*Let us hold fast
the confession of our hope
without wavering,
for he who promised is faithful.*
Hebrews 10:23

As winter lingers, I begin to get antsy and ready for springtime. I want to see more sunshine, hear the birds singing and watch them playing, as well as see and smell all the wonderful flowers. It seems like the more you focus on spring and want it to get here, the longer it takes getting here!

I am a biblical counselor and have counseled a good number of women and girls throughout the years, formally and informally. A recurring theme in these sessions—regardless of age, race, socioeconomic level, or marital status—is impatience during the wait.

Teenage girls are tired of being treated like

children and want their parents to allow them the privileges of adulthood. While these privileges vary from person to person, she usually means that her parents will not allow her to do what she wants to do, stay out as late as she wants with whomever she wants, for instance. Rarely do these teenagers talk about the responsibility that being an adult brings: paying a mortgage or rent, buying groceries, gas, clothing, and so on. They are tired of waiting for the next phase of their lives to begin.

Many never-married single women in their late 20s and early 30s (and older) don't understand why they haven't yet found a husband. After all, they know someone who found a husband and she hasn't even been faithful to God. They are tired of waiting for the next phase of their life to begin.

Many single women of all ages wish others in their church treated them like adults, capable of being responsible and making wise decisions, and of being trusted in appropriate leadership roles. They sense that others view them as incomplete because they aren't married. Whether their feelings are based on fact or personal insecurities, they are tired of waiting for the next phase of their lives to begin.

Young married women long to give birth and be a mom. They express their frustration and even anger that they have not yet conceived. They feel ridicule (imagined or real) from mothers who are their age. Sometimes, they even heap ridicule on themselves. They are tired of waiting for the next phase of their life to begin.

Today's passage tells us to "hold fast" to hope. The idea here is clinging to hope in the same way a child clings to his mom. The New Living Translation says, "hold tightly … to the hope." So, our responsibility when we are tired of waiting is to cling to or hold tightly to hope.

For those mentioned earlier, it does not necessarily mean teenagers will get adult privileges, never-married single women will get married, or married women will conceive a child. It does mean that regardless of what comes into your life, God is with you and will enable you to walk through it, not in drudgery and fear, but in hopeful confidence that God is in control.

There are many Scripture passages to which you can go for a definition of hope. One of my many favorites is, "We have this as a sure and steadfast anchor of the soul" (Hebrews 6:19a).

I explain hope as the anchor of God's presence in us that compels and propels us to keep believing in the power of God. It enables us to endure and walk confidently during the waiting periods and trials.

This hope is also for eternity. As Christ-followers, we trust that God has redeemed us and that we will spend eternity in heaven praising God.

If your hope is in anything or anyone other than God Himself, there is no basis for your hope. It is useless.

The chorus of an old hymn, "My Anchor Holds" by W. C. Martin, speaks to the hope that anchors us while we persevere in waiting and during trials:

> And it holds, my anchor holds:
> Blow your wildest, then, O gale,
> On my bark, so small and frail;
> By His grace I shall not fail,
> For my anchor holds, my anchor holds.

Amen! Do not despair, spring is coming!

Prayer: Heavenly Father, we are impatient as we wait for the seasons in nature and in our lives to change. As we walk in obedience to Your commands, teach us to cling to the hope for our future here on earth and for eternity. When situations seem hopeless, remind us to hold on to You, the Anchor of our Hope. In Jesus' name, Amen.

Thought for the Day: Hope in God anchors our soul firmly and securely. In whom or in what are you placing your hope?

Day 5: The Winter is Past

by Harriet
Read: Isaiah 43:18-21

See! The winter is past;
the rains are over and gone.
Flowers appear on the earth;
the season of singing has come,
the cooing of doves is heard in our land.
Song of Solomon 2:11-12 (NIV)

"See! the winter is past!" What a refreshing verse and how appropriate it is for this last devotion of a winter devotional book. During the winter, nature rests. It rests but it doesn't die, though it could sometimes appear that way. Grass puffs out and browns to protect itself from the cold. Trees shed and become bare as if a giant eraser has been used on them. They clean off all their clutter, making ready for the new growth that will come in the spring. But now, at the end of that season, the days began to grow longer and warmer. That new growth for which we have been eagerly waiting is just around the corner.

There's an anticipation to the end of winter—a waiting for what God is going to do in the world around us. Spiritually, we might not even realize we're at the end of winter if we have been seeking the Lord's direction. We'll find peace and contentment in our waiting and will only recognize that spring has sprung after noticing the grass is turning a bit greener and a few dandelions are beginning to sprout. Finally, our anticipation of abundance to come bursts into realization that is happening.

This time of year, when the winter ends in America and we begin experiencing spring, the rainy season is also beginning in tropical countries like Nigeria. It never gets old to me. The world going from barren to lush almost feels miraculous to me, no matter where it occurs.

I once heard an essay written by a missionary aunt who is no longer alive entitled, "Shades of Green." In it, she described Nigeria in the rainy season in absolutely beautiful terms. I heard the essay read aloud at talent night at a missionary reunion I attend annually, and I loved it the minute I heard it. It brought back a flood of vivid memories of the land of my childhood that I love so much.

She described standing at the window of her house in Nigeria looking at the lush outside world after a rain, saying it looked like the colors had been squeezed from an artist's color tubes in various shades of green, from the green on the mango trees that were so dark they almost looked black, to bright blue-greens of the ferns.

As a child, I remember how happy we all were when the rains finally came again, and our dry, dusty world changed to green almost overnight. I get that same excitement in America when the trees bud and the grass begins to turn green. I love this change of seasons from winter to spring.

Isaiah 43:19 says, "See, I am doing a new thing! Now it springs up; do you not perceive it?" In this passage, God is not speaking of flowers popping up from the barren ground; rather He is speaking of a new work He was doing among His people. This time of year, when the winter is ending, and spring is just beginning to change everything in the world around us is such a good reminder of God's ability to make all things new. The spiritual implications are everywhere. We just need to notice. The same God who can make flowers bloom where the earth had been barren, can make people's lives blossom when they too had once been barren.

Have you experienced a spiritual winter? Have you had a time in your life where it seemed nothing bloomed, no fruit was being produced? Remember there is actually a lot happening to the world during the cold barren days of winter. God is making it ready for an abundance that can only happen after the world has rested and cleaned away all its clutter from the previous year. May God give us eyes to spot the work He is doing all around us.

Prayer: Heavenly Father, You are a miracle-working God. You are in the business of changing lives and bringing forth fruit where there had been no fruit. Teach us to see the work You are doing in and around us. In Jesus' name, Amen.

Thought for the Day: God is doing a new thing. It's beginning to spring up all around you. The winter is past. Train your eyes to see what God is doing.

Acknowledgments

We are grateful to the Lord for allowing us to collaborate on another devotional. The Lord has been gracious to plant seeds of friendship in our hearts when we were young children and to deepen those bonds through our relationship with Him and with each other.

We are thankful for Harriet's daughter, Kristin Michael, for creating the beautiful illustrations you will find throughout the devotional.

We are grateful for the support, guidance, and encouragement our Nigerian missionary-kid cousin, Baker Hill provided during the process of writing this devotional.

We appreciate the contribution of Angela Maddox who helped us refine our manuscript.

We also want to thank Chautona Havig and for the beautiful cover design concept.

We are indebted to our friend and publisher, Marji Laine Clubine, for her encouragement and direction as she worked tirelessly helping us to bring this devotional to print.

About the Authors

Harriet E. Michael

Harriet E. Michael was born in Joinkrama, Nigeria, deep in the African Jungle in the Niger River Delta, where her father served as the only missionary doctor at that station. A few years later, the mission moved the family to a larger hospital in Ogbomoso. Co-author, Shirley Crowder and her family lived right across the dirt road. The two children became constant playmates. Today they continue to enjoy their lifelong friendship.

Harriet is a multi-published, award-winning writer and speaker. She has authored or co-authored six books (five non-fiction and one novel) with several more under contract for future release. She is also a prolific freelance writer having penned over 200 articles, devotions, and stories. Her work has appeared in publications by Focus on the Family, David C. Cook, Lifeway, Standard Publishing, *Chicken Soup for the Soul*, *The Upper*

Room, Judson Press, Bethany House, and more. When not writing, she loves speaking to women's groups about prayer and other topics as well as teaching workshops at writers' conferences.

She and her husband of over 40 years have four children and two grandchildren. When not writing, she enjoys substituting at a Christian school near her home, gardening, cooking, and traveling.

Follow her on:

Facebook: /harrietmichaelauthor

Blog: www.harrietemichael.blogspot.com

Amazon: amazon.com/author/harrietemichael

Shirley Crowder

Shirley Crowder was born in a mission guest house under the shade of a mango tree in Nigeria, West Africa, where her parents served as missionaries. She and co-author Harriet E. Michael grew up together on the mission field and have been life-long friends. Shirley is passionate about disciple-making, which is manifested in and through a myriad of ministry opportunities: biblical counseling, teaching Bible studies, writing, and music.

She is a biblical counselor and is commissioned by and serves on the national Advisory Team for The Addiction Connection. Several of her articles have appeared in "Paper Pulpit" in *The Gadsden Times'* Faith section, and in a David C. Cook publication. She also writes articles for Life Bible Study, Woman's Missionary Union, InspiredPrompt.com and TheAddictionConnection.org. She has authored or co-authored six books.

Shirley has spiritual children, grandchildren, and even great-grandchildren serving the Lord in various ministry and secular positions throughout the world.

Follow her on:
Facebook: /ShirleyCrowderAuthor
Twitter: @ShirleyJCrowder
Blog: www.throughthelensofScripture.com
Amazon: amazon.com/author/shirleycrowder

Also by the Authors

The Prayer Project
by Harriet and Shirley

Non-fiction from Entrusted Books

In this first book in the "Hope Rising Bible Series," Andrea Thom digs deep into the truths found in the book of Ruth. Her discoveries encourage women seeking meaning from difficult times and direction in the path on which the Lord has placed them.

Every week across America, single members filter into their local congregations to worship, minister, and serve alongside their brothers and sisters in Christ. Pastors and church leaders, many long married, often find themselves ill-equipped to understand the particular relational, emotional, and spiritual needs of long-term Christian singles. Worse, they're unaware that they're underequipped. Married church members, though sympathetic to the needs of their single friends, nevertheless struggle to bridge the divide.

Written by a dedicated Christ-follower and long-term Christian single, The Proper Care and Feeding of Singles addresses the issues with humor and grace, offering practical solutions to strengthen the bonds of love and fellowship within local congregations.

Hymns and Poetry

"All Things Bright and Beautiful,"
     Cecil Frances Alexander
"As From the Winter Sky," James Montgomery
"Awake, My Soul, Stretch Every Nerve,"
     Philip Doddridge
"For the Beauty of The Earth,"
     Folliott S. Pierpoint
"Give Me Jesus," Fanny J. Crosby
"His Eye is On the Sparrow," Civilla D. Martin
"Holy, Holy, Holy! Lord God Almighty,"
     Reginal Heber
"In The Morning When I Rise (Give Me Jesus),"
     African American spiritual
"It Is Well with My Soul,"
     Horatio Gates Spafford
"Joy Unspeakable," Barney E. Warren
"Kept by the Power of God," Barney E. Warren
"Moment by Moment," Daniel Whittle
"My Anchor Holds," W. C. Martin
"Nothing But the Blood," Robert Lowry
"O God Our Help in Ages Past," Isaac Watts
"Since Jesus Came into My Heart,"
     Rufus H. McDaniel
"Sun of My Soul," John Keble
"Tell It to Jesus," Edmund S. Lorenz
"The Heavens are Telling the Glory of God,"
     Joseph Haydn
"The Holly and the Ivy," Anonymous.
"The Love of God," Richard M. Lehman
"The North Wind Doth Blow," Anonymous
"The Voices of Creation," Valdimar Briem
"There Is Sunshine in My Soul Today,"
     Eliza Hewitt
"This is My Father's World," Maltbie D. Babcock

"'Tis Winter Now," Samuel Longfellow
"Trust and Obey," John H. Sammis
"Trusting Jesus," Edgar P. Stites
"We Rest on Thee," Edith G. Cherry
"What a Friend We Have in Jesus,"
      Joseph M. Scriven
"While Shepherds Watched Their Flocks by Night,"
      tune by George Frederick Handel
"Whiter Than Snow," James Nicholson

Thank you
for reading our books!

If you enjoyed this devotional,
please consider returning to its
purchase page and leaving a review!

Look for other books
published by

Entrusted Books
an Imprint of
Write Integrity Press

www.WriteIntegrity.com

Made in the USA
Lexington, KY
05 November 2019

56484158R00199